PURPOSE UNLOCKED

Discovering Your Mission
to Impact the World

PETER OWUSU ANSAH

ISBN: 978-9988-2-3453-9

To invite Apostle Peter to speak at your seminars, conferences, church or school events,
contact him on:
Mobile: +233244249687 / 0504101374
Email: peteronpurpose1@yahoo.com
Edited, by Buabeng Communications
Contact: 0246 88 26 32/ 0576 533 249
Email: jeremiahbuabeng@ymail.com
Printed by Victory Printz Ventures
(0244 146 758 / 0208 877 197)
Cover Page Designed by
Crown Concept (0270 565 089)

CONTENTS

DEDICATION

I dedicate this book to the almighty God for his divine enablement that has made this book a reality. I am highly indebted to you Lord. You have been so faithful to me in every aspect of my life.

YOUR NAME BE FOREVER PRAISED.

I also dedicate this book to all young people who are making impact in people's lives and destinies by carrying out their God-given assignments in their chosen careers, professions, ministries and callings, in the face of all oppositions and struggles. I am one of you so I know how it feels. Don't give up. Fight on comrades. God is on your side.

Finally, I dedicate this book to my wife for supporting and understanding my ministry. Cherry, my prayer for you is that you will identify and fulfill God's assignment for your life and become all that God intends for you.

ACKNOWLEDGMENTS

All glory and honour to the unchangeable changer, Almighty God, keeper and source of all creation. I am grateful to God for all His mercies and grace upon my life. I have come this far because of the blessings of God through his son Jesus Christ and the presence of the Holy Spirit. Thank you Lord God Almighty for inspiring us to inspire your people through writing.

I am highly indebted to my parents, Charity Osei Boamah and Augustine Otoo. I thank God for your lives. A big thank you to my foster father Mr. Eric Amoah for your love and care. God in his infinite wisdom chose you to be the loins and womb that introduced me into this world. God richly bless you.

Much thanks to all the great men and women of God through whom God has shaped my life and ministry. God bless you all. Permit me to single out Rev. Fr. Emmanuel Obeng Codjoe and Fr. Hillary Agbenosi for your immense support and encouragement. I am indebted to my pastor Very Rev. Fr John Benyah Mensah for his love and support over the years. I cannot but pause to thank God for the lives of Prophet Diallo Godfield Opong, Rev. Kyere Duodu and Apostle Daniel Clad for the impact you've had on my life. Many thanks to Mr. and Mrs. Paul Otoo and Mr. and Mrs. Emmanuel Tamakloe for your guidance. Rev. Fr. Maxwell Quaye, you've been a friend and a spiritual director to me, I am very grateful.

Much thanks to Mrs. Theresah Osei Bonsu who blessed me with a laptop a year ago, this kind gesture was a milestone in my writing ministry. I am also grateful to Charles Adiyiah Kusi Jnr, Victor Gborglah, Madam Lucy Peprah and Valeria Mensah for your seed offering into my ministry. God bless you all abundantly.

I want to acknowledge my wife Cherry, for understanding and supporting my ministry. It takes the support of a special woman (wife) for a man (husband) to have a fruitful ministry.

To my three good friends Gabriel Amofah, Michael Ofori and Oscar Akotey, I can't thank you enough for all your support and love.

My sincere thanks to friends and relatives like Miss Maxima Missodey, Mrs. Harriet Baffoe-White, Miss Evelyn Avevor, Bro. John Ahiakpa, Mr. Joseph Osei Barfi, for proofreading and editing this work. You did a good job. I appreciate Jeremiah Buabeng for the professional input you made on this project. To Godwin Martey, I say a big thank you for the permission to use your write-up.

Finally, to all friends and loved ones who have contributed in diverse ways to the success of this work.

May God richly bless you all.

FOREWORD

After my ordination as a Catholic Priest, one of the lay people in the Church whose ministry has impacted greatly on my apostolate is the author of this book, *'Purpose Unlocked'*. Although a nurse by profession and a married man with one child he has found great joy in the Lord by pursuing his ministry as a music minister, a preacher and a writer. Peter Owusu Ansah makes an important and tremendously valuable contribution to the discovery of a person's God-given purpose. Using his own life experiences and that of others, Peter shows how they have journeyed with the Lord in seeking and fulfilling their God-given purpose.

Many a time, in the course of my priestly ministry, I meet a lot of people who although have graduated from the tertiary institutions are still struggling to identify and pursue their purposes in life. Indeed many more people find themselves in this domain. This book will surely journey with you and help you in unearthing your potentials. I therefore deem this book as helpful and worth reading and I thank Peter for authoring it.

This awesome book is biblically rooted, practical, simple, interesting to read and to comprehend. It will interest you to know that Christians of all denominations and non-Christians alike will find this book very beneficial.

I highly consider this book as a great asset and I recommend it to all people. I am very sure that they will find it worth their while to peruse and digest its contents. May God equip you with the grace needed to understand His purpose for you even as you read this book and may He fill you with the ability to put into action all the plans He has for you, in the matchless name of Jesus, Amen. Jesus is Lord.

Rev. Fr. Emmanuel Teresa Obeng Codjoe
Solemnity of the Immaculate Conception, 2015

INTRODUCTION

"When life has no intentional destiny; when it has no bivouac, no habour, no ideal, it is full of mediocrity and tendium. It then becomes completely exteriorized with consequent loss of much power and peace." (Life Is Worth Living By: Archbishop Fulton J. Sheen)

"About 8 years ago, I took a decision that was directly in line with the will of God for my life, it was exactly my purpose. Somehow I had known that entrepreneurship was my calling. I was working as a Head of Section in a Polytechnic and lectured some courses too. Sincerely, it wasn't bad, the pay was good considering the standard of living then and also for the fact that I was staying with my uncle so I wasn't paying utilities. But every day, as I woke up and dressed to work, I usually felt this deep sense of dissatisfaction. My most dreaded moments were Sunday nights, ah! I will feel this "down-heartedness" because it's almost dawn and I had to go out again to do what I really knew wasn't my calling. I gathered the courage one day and decided to start something new. I didn't just quit overnight. I knew that I had to deny myself a lot of comforts if I really wanted to pursue that purpose-driven life. I very much believed in the Latin maxim; "Non sine pulvere palma" which means, "the prize cannot be won without effort." However, I also felt that, it is a necessary part to plan my exit in such a way as to mitigate the impact of the aftershocks that will naturally follow from my decision. Today, I have realized there is a beautiful life out there.

Material wealth is good since I believe it is a blessing from God, however, I must concede that, the deep inner sense of fulfillment, and the knowledge that I am charting a life of destiny, are priceless and far outweigh the joy I derive from material blessings.

There is still a huge mountain to climb. Perhaps bigger than previously, however, the difference is that, the challenges I face now are more exciting to me and so I face them with passion. When man finds his essence of being, life becomes worth living. There is real freedom in this mindset because you see yourself as being in harmony with creation.

Now, understand this, your purpose is not necessarily Entrepreneurship. Infact, you may be running a business and be out of purpose. You will find out that you are a frustrated and an unhappy CEO and you have a heavy burden waking up and heading to the office. You may end up being happier being employed by Bill Gates and even have more success than you will ever do owning your own business. If you worked with Bill Gates and owned 1% of Microsoft, with deep sense of peace, isn't that better?

If you are teaching in a School, but you know deep down your heart that you have always wanted to be a medical Doctor, please, re-direct your sail, pray for guidance from God and start finding ways to get back to medical school. Of what use is it living a life and growing to be 80 years yet unfulfilled?

You may even be a Church staff, and you know that you are not happy. You are not using your skills enough. You are not seeing personal growth and development, quit! Don't let the Pastor brainwash you, he is fulfilling his own dream and purpose and he is happy, God is happy with him, so wake up and go and discover why you were born. It is not difficult, usually your heart is already longing and groaning in that direction. You are growing old, don't think you have time, every second is irredeemable.

Please, I beseech you therefore brethren, that you take that bold step of faith, quit living a rented purpose, be the landlord of your own dreams, it is not about money at all, it is about personal purpose, happiness, deep sense of fulfillment, and like me, even when you are broke temporarily, you will still be happy. Most times you actually hardly ever get broke again, because there is abundance waiting for you in your purpose." (Paraphrased and rephrased from a Facebook posted 9th April, 2015 by Godwin Martey, CEO, Websoft Solutions, Ghana).

"To have passion, to have a dream, to have a purpose in life. And there are three components to that purpose, one is to find out who you really are, to discover God, the second is to serve other human beings, because we are here to do that and the third is to express your unique talent and when you are expressing your unique talents you lose track of time." Deepak Chopra (American author and public speaker)

What do you aspire to become in the near future?

What is your career? Where do you see yourself in the next 15 years? What are you good at, naturally? What are the things that bring out the best in you? What are your natural gifts, abilities and talents? Which direction do you think God is leading you in terms of career, ministry and your calling? Do you enjoy talking or looking for opportunities to make your voice heard? Do you love mathematics and the sciences or you have a flair for the social sciences? Do you have a natural flair for drama, music, dance or you love the creative arts in general? Have you come to that place of deep conviction as to what exactly you want to be known for in your lifetime? What do you exist for? Why do you think God created you? What is that one thing that defines you?

Simply put, what is your purpose in life? Pause and think for a moment!

I believe there are a number of people who are not fulfilled in their chosen careers, professions, business enterprises and ministries. And this could be largely the case because most people haven't taken the responsibility of identifying what their true purpose on earth is. People live their lives anyhow. They don't have any sense of direction in life. Anything goes for them. They live their lives on chance and luck. They are not strategic about their choices. They follow the crowd blindly. They are aimless in life. They have no specific motivation for the kind of career and academic path they take. They are simply not purposeful in life. There are yet so many successful people who are not fulfilled and exasperated in life and they feel a vacuum in their lives after all their accomplishment. They feel a sense of emptiness in them. Why? The answer is that, they haven't fulfilled that for which they were created. Unfortunately, for those who have identified their God-given purposes, they have not been able to fully fulfill their purposes due to certain challenges they've had to endure.

A PURPOSE-DRIVEN LIFE IS THE ONLY SOURCE OF TRUE FULFILMENT IN LIFE

"When are we most happy? When we do that for which we are made, as the microphone is happy when it does that for which it was made. Then there is a thrill and a romance to life." (Life Is Worth Living By: Archbishop Fulton J. Sheen)

Life without a purpose is like going on a journey without a known destination. Imagine how such a journey would be.

"PURPOSE UNLOCKED" is going to take you on a journey of identifying your God-given purpose on earth. It will provide you with basic practical guidelines that will aid you to identify your God-given purpose. The book tries to bring out certain qualities and dispositions that the reader must adopt in order to be able to live a more meaningful and purposeful life. You would be inspired to be a winner in life! You would be challenged to go for your best in life. You would be equipped with tools that will unleash the champion in you no matter where you find yourself presently in life. 'Purpose Unlocked' makes use of illustrations from the Bible to help you discover your purpose and the true essence of living a purposeful life.

Discovering your purpose is very crucial to your very existence because almost everything about your life revolves around your purpose. Your choice of career, profession, course of study and even choice of marriage partner to some extent has a direct or indirect impact on your life's mission. There is a saying that, "if you don't know where you are going any route can take you there."(Myles Munroe). That would be an awful situation.

There are so many young people and even adults who are confused in life because they haven't taken time to identify their purpose on earth. Others went to colleges and universities with no idea of what they desire to become in the future. It is sad to find people who change from 'job A' to 'job B' almost every year because they lack the basic knowledge about what they exist for.

This is total confusion. Such a life is in chaos but they've not realised it. You can't achieve anything tangible and fulfilling with this kind of lifestyle. Many people are actually living out their lives on trial and error basis. That's a dangerous and risky disposition.

You must have a clearer picture about how you want your future to look like. You can't leave your destiny to chance and fate. You must be intentional and purposeful about your life.

A clear vision about your assignment on earth will bring you the following benefits;

1. It makes you focus and gives you a sense of direction.
2. It guides you as to how to and where to channel your resources.
3. It helps you live a fulfilled life.
4. It helps you assess your life well.
5. It helps you identify your strengths and weaknesses.
6. It makes you a master of your own destiny and guides you in your decisions and choices.
7. It makes you a useful member of the society.

You dare not miss this truth about your existence on earth because the consequences of not knowing it could be risky. It is a must for you to identify and live out your purpose to the max. You don't have any other option if you really want to make a lasting impact in your lifetime. For some people, the concept of purpose doesn't even ring a bell. They have no idea about what purpose is about. Don't worry if you find yourself in any of these categories. The subsequent pages will help you out. By the time you are done reading this book, you would be steps ahead so far as purpose discovery and fulfilment is concerned.

Parents and guardians must not blindly guide our wards and children into fields and courses they have no passion or interest in. They should be able to figure out where their academic strengths lie. Parents must guide their children or wards to make career and academic choices based on their natural talents and abilities. The Bible says in Proverbs 22:6 that: "Train up the child in the way he should go, and when he is old he will not depart from it."Never should we force our wards to pursue programmes that are not in sync with their passions. This book will guide you to help your child make the best choices about career and academics.

You have in your hand a book that will turn your world around. You are about to unravel mysteries about your own life. You are about to discover the potentials that God has placed in you. The book is good for people of all age groups but it generally addresses the needs of young people who are hungry to discover and execute their God-given assignments fully. This book will teach, motivate, challenge, guide and spur you on to identify and pursue your God-given assignment to the fullest.

CHAPTER ONE

WHAT IS PURPOSE?

"Everything in life has a purpose. Everyone on this planet was born with and for a purpose. It is this purpose that is the only source of meaning. Without purpose, life is an experiment or a haphazard journey that results in frustration, disappointment and failure. Without purpose, life is subjective, or it's a trial and error game that is ruled by environmental influences and the circumstances of the moment. Likewise, in the absence of purpose, time has no meaning, energy has no reason and life has no precision. Therefore, it is essential that we understand and discover our purpose in life so that we can experience an effective, full and rewarding life."(Dr. Myles Munroe).

"Man is called to a fullness of life which far exceeds the dimensions of his earthly existence, because it consists in sharing the very life of God." (Catholic theology of the body and Teachings of Pope John Paul II)

What exactly is 'purpose'?

1. The object toward which one strives or for which something exists: an aim or a goal.

2. The reason for which something exists or is done, made, used, etc.

3. An intended or desired result, end, aim or goal.

4. The original intent for the creation of a thing.

5. The original reason for the existence of a thing.

6. The end for which the means exist.

7. The cause for the creation of a thing.

8. The desired result that initiates production

9. The need that makes a manufacturer produce a specific product.

10. The destination that prompts the journey.

11. The objective of the subject.

12. The aspiration for the inspiration.

13.   The object one wills or resolves to have.

Purpose, therefore, in my view, in simple terms refers to 'the use or usefulness of a particular thing, object or a person or group of persons, the reason for which something or a person exists or was created.' The pen was basically made to write. The purpose of a pen is simply to write. The fact that you can use a pen to rule out a straight line on a piece of paper doesn't necessarily turn the pen into a simple measuring rule. A pen is a pen and it should be used for writing; **PERIOD.** In the mind of the manufacturer, the pen has a purpose and that purpose is the function of writing. The inventor or manufacturer of a pen intended it to be used primarily for writing.

In the same manner, every human being was created by God for a specific purpose. Jeremiah 1:5 says "Before I formed you in the womb I knew you: Before you were born I set you apart; I appointed you as a prophet to the nations." This means that God had already spelt out your supposed mission on earth before you were born. God had an intention for creating you. He had a particular use for your existence on this planet. He created you to meet a particular need and that need is your purpose. He made you to solve specific problems of mankind and human life.

THAT SOLUTION OR SET OF SOLUTIONS IS YOUR PURPOSE.

The fact that you enrolled and graduated from the teacher training college doesn't necessarily make you a teacher. For all you know you were probably destined to be an international soccer star. God made you to accomplish a specific task on earth. He designed you specially, uniquely and specifically for that particular mission. Your make-up is originally framed to help you accomplish that particular task. An individual's purpose in my own opinion is, 'that assignment that God created a person to fulfill in a lifetime.' If you had no business coming to this earth, God wouldn't have bothered to create you in the first place. You are on a mission here on earth. There is a specific path you must follow in order to live a life worthwhile and meaningful. God didn't create you just to grow up, get schooled, find a good job, marry, have children and then die without making a mark with your life. You were created to leave behind a legacy. Your purpose is your life's assignment. Your purpose is your mission.

TYPES OF PURPOSE

(Inspired by Dr. Mensa Otabil)

The Ultimate / Primary Purpose

Specific / Secondary Purpose

General Purpose

Intended Purpose

Invented Purpose

Inverted Purpose

THE ULTIMATE/PRIMARY PURPOSE

"Everyone who is called by my name, And whom I have created for My glory, Whom I have formed, even whom I have made," (Isaiah 43:7).

Our purpose in life, as God originally created man, is to:

1. Glorify God and enjoy fellowship with Him (salvation).
2. Have good relationships with others.
3. Work.
4. Have dominion over the earth.

"You are worthy, O Lord to receive glory and honour and power: for you have created all things, and for your pleasure they are and were created." (Rev 4:11).

The Bible is very clear as to what our purpose in life should be. Certain men and women in both the Old and New Testaments sought and discovered life's purpose. Solomon, the wisest man who ever lived (Apart from Jesus), discovered the futility of life when it is lived only for this world. He gives these concluding remarks in the book of Ecclesiastes: *"Here is the conclusion of the matter: Fear God and keep his commandments, for this is the whole duty of man. For God will bring every deed into judgment, including every hidden thing, whether it is good or evil" (Ecclesiastes 12:13-14).* Solomon says that life is all about honoring God with our thoughts and life and thus keeping His commandments, for one day we will stand before Him in judgment. Part of our purpose in life is to fear God and obey Him.

According to the Bible, our purpose, the reason we are here, is for God's glory. In other words, our purpose is to praise God, worship Him, to proclaim His greatness, and to accomplish His will. This is what glorifies Him. Therefore, in this we find that God has given us a reason for our existence, a meaning for our existence. We were created by Him, according to His desire; and our lives are to be lived for Him so that we might accomplish what He has for us to do. When we trust the one who has made us, who works all things after the counsel of His will *(Ephesians 1:11),* then we are able to live a life of purpose. How the particulars of that purpose are expressed is up to the individual.

The apostle Paul talked about all he had achieved religiously before being confronted by the risen Christ, and he concluded that all of it was like a pile of manure compared to the excellence of knowing Christ Jesus. *In Philipians 3:9-10*, Paul says that he wants nothing more than to know Christ and *"be found in Him,"* to have His righteousness and to live by faith in Him, even if it meant suffering and dying. Paul's purpose was knowing Christ, having a righteousness obtained through faith in Him, and living in fellowship with Him, even when that brought on suffering *(2 Timothy 3:12)*. Ultimately, he looked for the time when he would be a part of the *"resurrection from the dead."* Is your life glorifying God?

"Scripture and Tradition never cease to teach and celebrate this fundamental truth: "The world was made for the glory of God." St. Bonaventure explains that God created all things "not to increase his glory, but to show it forth and to communicate it", for God has no other reason for creating than his love and goodness: "Creatures came into existence when the key of love opened his hand." The First Vatican Council explains. (Catechism of the Catholic Church: Number 293)

SPECIFIC/SECONDARY PURPOSE

The word 'specific' means; specified, precise, or particular. Therefore specific purpose means; the kind of purpose that is precise and specified. In as much as we desire to achieve so much with our lives for the good of the society and for personal fulfilment, we should not lose sight of the fact that sometimes, we may not be called to follow the general purpose of the population, rather God may be preparing us to execute a specific assignment. It is better to be a master in one thing than to be a jack of all trades and master of none. You may be called into general church ministry, however, it is your responsibility to find out from God your specific area of calling. Is it youth ministry? Is it children's ministry? Is the Lord calling you into the music ministry? Even if you are called to the music ministry, which specific role is God requiring of you to play. You need to find out. The fact that God predestined you to be a businessman doesn't guarantee that you will succeed in every area of business. No, it doesn't work like that. Is it agro-business, real estates, imports and exports, etc.? Are you called into the health sector? Which area of specialisation do you have the flair and strength for, is it medicine, nursing, physiotherapy, paediatrics, mental health, etc.? What is your specific purpose on earth? *Which One Thing Are You Here On Earth For?*

GENERAL PURPOSE

This kind of purpose is related to the ultimate purpose. Some purposes are not specific to particular people and places. General purpose almost apply to all human beings. We have all been called to love, serve and worship the one true God. We all have a mandate to love our neighbours no matter their colour, race, religion, language, etc. As Christians, it is our general purpose to evangelise and win souls into the kingdom of God. It is our duty as human beings to remain faithful stewards and custodians of creation. God expects us to keep our environment clean and protect the dignity and worth of the environment. These are all examples of general purposes that are not peculiar to certain people, groups of people and locations. It is my prayer that we would not just follow selfish, parochial and ambitious aspirations, but we would yield to the intended purposes God has destined for each of us. That in all our endeavours we will seek to please God and none other.

INTENDED PURPOSE

This is the original purpose that God had in mind for each individual human being. It is the original intent of God concerning you and I. God had a certain clear picture of how our future ought to look like. As already said, we are his end-products and he is our Creator. We are like the cast in a play and God is the playwright. There is a certain path that our lives must follow. That path is God's roadmap for our destinies. For example, God's intended purpose for Jesus Christ on earth was for him to come and die to save mankind. Anything apart from this would have rendered Jesus' life and mission a total failure. If God's intended purpose for you was to become a medical doctor and out of ignorance and or disobedience you end up becoming a lawyer, although your law practice may be useful to you and the society, in the sight of God you are below God's standard because you missed his original plan for your life.

INVENTED PURPOSE

To invent means to originate or create as a product of one's own ingenuity. Intended purpose is created by God while invented purpose is created by man. In other words, it is a result of man's own innovation. Apart from God's intended plan and purpose for our lives, we sometimes pursue certain careers and vocations out of sheer personal ambitions and aspirations. Such pursuits may not necessarily be bad in themselves but they are certainly not the best for the fact that they are outside God's purpose for our lives. God is the only giver of purpose and not man. Man can only discover purpose. Man cannot create purpose. God is the only inventor of true purpose. In 2 Samuel 7:1-29, King David at a point in his reign wanted to build a temple for the Lord, in other words, David wanted to invent a purpose but God stopped him because his son Solomon was the one God intended to build him a dwelling place of worship. These are bitter pills we must be ready to swallow in life if we desire the backing of God in the decisions and choices we make in life. It is better and safer to follow God's intended purpose for your life and remain a village star and be pleasing to God than to disobediently follow your own invented purpose and gain international recognition. If God is not in it, it doesn't please him, it had better not been done. *"Many are the plans in a man's heart, but it is the Lord's purpose that prevails." (Prov. 19:21).*

In Genesis, the eleventh chapter, the people of Babel decided to build a city and a tower that would reach to the heaven. God was displeased by this agenda so he set confusion among the people by confounding their language. *"And the Lord came down to see the city and the tower, which the children of men builded. And the Lord said, Behold, the people are one, and they have all one language; and this they begin to do: and now nothing will be restrained from them, which they have imagined to do. Come, let us go down and there confound their language, that they may not understand one another's speech. So the Lord scattered them abroad from upon the face of all the earth: and they ceased building the city."*

(Gen. 11:5-8). For a moment it looked as if the people of Babel were on a good cause until God set confusion among them. I believe they thought they were pursuing a great project, unknown to them, God was actually against them because they wanted to make a name for themselves. Sometimes, God allows people to follow their own selfish and vain purposes. Some may even seem successful in the sight of men, but once it fails to get the approval of God, such a purpose cannot be termed as God-ordained. ***Don't Be Like The People Of Babel.***

INVERTED PURPOSE

To invert means to turn upside down, to reverse in order, position, direction, or relationship. This happens when we follow God's plan for our lives but in a different direction, time, place and for that matter follow it at all. For example, if God calls someone to become a preacher as a catholic priest in an African country and that fellow rather chooses to become a pastor of the Presbyterian Church in the United States of America, that fellow has inverted his purpose. What it would mean is that, although such a person may be endowed with the qualities of a preacher and be bearing fruits, he or she is still operating in error because of the change in direction, nature and location of purpose. Most times people get caught up in this kind of web because of fear and the uncertainties of the future. A classical biblical example is the story of Jonah. ***"Now the word of the Lord came to Jonah son of Amittai: Go to the greatest city of Nineveh and preach against it, because its wickedness has come up before me. But Jonah ran away from the Lord and headed for Tarshish. He went down to Joppa, where he found a ship bound for that port. After paying the fare, he went aboard and sailed for Tarshish to flee from the Lord." (Jonah 1:1-3).*** In fact this story of Jonah rightly fits for both invented and inverted purposes. Anytime we choose such a path, the end result will obviously be one of doom.

TANGIBLES OF PURPOSE

Within your purpose are solutions to many problems.
There is a puzzle that only you can solve.
There is a song that only you can sing.

There is a book that only you can write.

There is an idea that only you can conceive.

There is a thought that only you can perceive.

There is a house that only you can build.

There is an edifice that only you can design.

There are people that only you can lead.

There is a government that only you can run.

There is a disease that only you can cure.

There is a place that only you can go.

There is a city that only you can build.

There is a programme / course that only you can develop.

There is a husband/wife that only you can marry.

Your failure to fully fulfill your God-given purpose will make our world incomplete. Failure to play your part in the game of life will make our team short of something. You matter, I matter, we all matter. You hold the key to a door and that key is your purpose. If you fail to find and use that particular key, you will deny a lot of people access to that door. Imagine our world today without the likes of Bill Gates and Steve Jobs. Imagine how incapacitated this planet earth would be without computers and all the technological inventions. The world would definitely have moved on but not at this rate without the advancements in technology.

You were created by God to accomplish a particular task and that task spells out your purpose. It is very possible you are the next Bill Gates. Yes, it is possible. Could it also be that God ordained and predestined you to be one of the most anointed men or women of God of our time? And even perhaps the next Pele? Your purpose is linked to your career. Your purpose is your calling. Your purpose is your mission. Until purpose is identified life cannot be well lived. I can't wait to see you pursue your God-given assignment to the full.

You are reading this book because at a point in my life I found out through experience and revelation that I was born to be a writer. May you be inspired as you read this book. I feel in my spirit that someone reading this book has the brains and economic know-how to address the socio-economic challenges of these times. Oh yes! I know I'm talking to a great business tycoon who will feed multitudes because God has wired you for that mandate. I am speaking to another 'Joseph' who will positively change the economic conditions of his generation. The world hasn't seen anything yet because I'm speaking to a 21st century inspirational musician who will impact the length and breadth of the planet with amazing tunes. I declare that you will fulfill your purpose in your lifetime.

PURPOSE IS DIFFERENT FROM MERE PERSONAL AMBITIONS

Whenever we talk about purpose, we place much emphasis on the fact that it is God-given. Purpose comes from God. It is God who shows and directs us to what we exist for. Your purpose is in God. Unfortunately people sometimes confuse *Personal Ambitions* with *God-given Purpose.* The two are not the same. A personal ambition could be an individual's pursuit and desire for certain accomplishments and achievements in life. Personal ambitions may or may not be from God. Personal ambitions are self-driven. They may not be necessarily borne out of divine conviction. For something to be considered as a God-given purpose, God must be the brain behind it. It will interest you to know that, a considerable number of the people who are being celebrated by the world today for certain accomplishments in certain spheres of life may not be approved by God. Why? It is because their achievements are not in line with God's blueprint for their lives and the good of humanity. There are a lot of businesses, marriages, industries, companies, NGOs, etc., that are doing so well, measuring by societal standards, but in the sight of God they need not to exist in the first place. It sounds debatable but that is the fact. ***The God-Factor*** cannot be washed down when dealing with the ***concept of purpose.***

For example, the members of terrorists-groups such as Al Qaeda and Boko haram have been able to carry out a number of atrocities against humanity. To them, they are successful because they've been able to accomplish their purpose, but every well-mannered human being will not consider the existence and activities of these groups as God-driven. Would you? A 'commercial sex worker' ***(prostitute)*** may consider her job to be lucrative and a great source of income to her and even her entire family. She may amass so much wealth through that and make a name in the society. She may even go into philanthropic missions with the proceeds of her prostitution. She may get headline stories in the news for her benevolence. Society may not even know that she is into prostitution, but can we consider her way of life as purpose and God-driven? Although she may be the bread winner of a number of people, the fact that she is into something that is illegal, immoral and ungodly alone disqualifies her lifestyle as being purpose-driven.

In fact, there are probably churches that have been established out of selfish ambition other than the will of God. There are businesses that have been established for parochial and dubious reasons. These to enrich the pockets of the owners. You can't categorise such institutions as being God-driven or purpose-driven.

NOT EVERY SUCCESS STORY IS A PURPOSE-STORY

Not every seemingly successful person or organization can be considered as *purposeful*. Society uses so many factors to define what success means. Factors such as how wealthy a person is, the influence of an individual or an organization on the society and the power an individual commands, among other things. Success in the sight of God is being able to do what He destined you for. At the end of life, we shall all stand before the Almighty God to give accounts of how we spent our lives on earth. Earthly approval is not equal to heaven's approval. Men may be praising you for certain accomplishments, yet to God, those accomplishments may be an eyesore. Any ambition that is not sanctioned by God is a personal ambition and not a divine one, whether that ambition is good or bad. That is the bitter truth.

May God reveal the blueprint for our lives to us. May he raise men and women who will not just follow any ambition but that which comes from God. May God grant unto us divine enlightenment to identify our God-given purposes and may he bless us with the physical and spiritual resources to fully accomplish them. May we not pursue our own agenda. May we not be seekers of societal approval and applause. On the contrary, may we be people who will seek out to pursue that which God has spelt out for us in his divine plan in Jesus name. Amen.

The Bible recounts that King David wanted to build a temple for God but the Lord restrained him (1 Chronicles 17:4). Why will God prevent him? Wasn't it a worthy cause? The answers are obvious. To God, Solomon, the son of David was rather destined to build God a dwelling place. It doesn't make sense but that is how God works. Sometimes, you can't just understand him. That's why the bible says his ways are not our ways, neither are his thoughts our thoughts. (Isaiah 55:8)

To man, success is any great achievement and accomplishment. But to God, true success is a life lived on and for purpose.

INDEED, "WHERE THERE IS NO PURPOSE, ABUSE IS INEVITABLE." *(Dr. Myles Munroe)* HEAR THIS CHILD OF GOD! (ASSIMILATE AND PERSONALISE THESE THOUGHTS)

You shall fulfill your purpose!

You are a solution to somebody's problem!

You are a key to a closed door!

You are the healing to a depressed nation!

You are an answer to so many unanswered questions!

You are God's channel of hope to a dying world!

You are God's instrument of peace to a chaotic world!

You are God's vessel of hope to a hopeless world!

You shall feed many!

You shall bring comfort and relief to nations!

You are another Christ to the world!

You are another saviour to the world!

You are another deliverer to the world!

You are the miracle the world needs!

You are a freedom fighter!

You are the mouthpiece of the marginalised!

You are an ambassador of Christ!

HOW DO I FIND MY PURPOSE?

I can feel by now you are beginning to ask questions about how you can identify this all-important God-given purpose. Begin the search now because it is right within you. Look around you. Listen to your inner man. Enquire of the lord. Pray about it. Seek elderly counsel. God is transforming you from an employee into an employer. Your destiny is far greater than just a common bank teller. You are a CEO of a multinational financial institution. Wake up. Rise up. Take off and let it happen.

Follow me as I lead you through the pages of the next chapters in a journey of purpose discovery.

CHAPTER TWO

ASK THE LORD

"Call to me and I will answer you, and show you great and mighty things which you do not know."
(Jeremiah 33:3)

How do I discover my purpose? You seem to be asking. You are not the only person asking this important question of a lifetime. Don't worry, you will soon find some useful answers as you read on. It will interest you to know that there are people in their 60s who are still asking this question, how pathetic. However, there's still hope for you once you have life. It is better to attempt living out your purpose than to die without discovering it at all. Various authors have prescribed different approaches in the journey of purpose discovery. I am inspired to help you discover your God-given purpose through the following chapters.

Your first point of call in your bid to identify your

purpose is to; ***ask the Lord***. Every divine assignment requires a divine relationship. You are a product of God. God manufactured (Created) you. You are a masterpiece of God. You are a work in progress by God. You are the product of the thought of God. God had you in mind from the beginning of creation. What am I trying to tell you? God is your first point of call in your search for purpose. Let's take the operating manual of any machine or electrical gadget for example, if you want to use a new devise effectively, you must first read the manufacturer's manual. This manual basically gives you a guide to how one can use the device appropriately and effectively. Failure to read and go by the manual's guidance may lead to an ineffective use of the device. It may even lead to the premature destruction of the device. In the same vein, God Almighty is the manufacturer and you are his product. In order to know your use and importance, you must seek the advice of the great manufacturer.

You didn't emanate from an ape as opined by some theorists. Going by the biblical account of creation, I can boldly say that you were created by the Almighty God of Abraham, Isaac and Jacob. You are not a product of the **Big Bang** theory. The truth of the matter is that you were created in the image and likeness of Yahweh *(Gen 1:26)*. It is worth noting that, of all the things God created according to biblical records, every creature was created through the spoken word of God.'Let there be this and let there be that' and 'there was this and there was that'. However, God the Father, Son and Holy Spirit thought it wise that they would take their time to make man(you and I) in their own image and likeness.*(Gen 1:26)*. My friend, you are very important to God. *Jeremiah 1:4-5* tells us that before you were a clot of blood in your mother's womb, God knew you already. Do you know that you are a product of billions of sperms that struggled to fertilise a single egg in your mother's womb? *You are a Champion and a Conqueror.*

The following scripture reference points to the fact that, anytime we call on God in prayer, he hears and answers us, *Jeremiah 33:3* and *Matthew 7:7*. I urge you to call on God in prayer concerning your purpose on earth. There is a God who knows your end from its beginning because He is the Alpha and the Omega. He is eternal and not bound by time. Before eternity, he was. He is the Omnipotent, Omniscient, and Omnipresent. Man is limited but God is limitless. Man is temporary but God is everlasting. I recommend to you this day that you go to God in prayer and you will definitely know your purpose.

Take some time off and retreat with the Lord. Begin to ask God some questions. God is your shepherd and He is ever willing to guide you in this quest. *Psalm 23* teaches of the relationship between us and God, God being our shepherd and we being his sheep. He's ever ready to lead us to the still waters of life. He is our rod which directs us when we don't know where to turn to. He will guide us even through the valley of the shadows of death. God's leadership is unfailing. He knows the plans he has for you and they are good, perfect and peaceful thoughts, to bring you to an expected end. God has already put down a plan for your life. He alone has the blueprint to your destiny.

He knows your very make-up. He sees every fiber, muscle, tissue and cell you are made of. He even knows the number of hairs on your head. (Luke 12:17)

There is a particular journey ahead of you in this life. It may be longer or shorter. It may be tougher or rosy. It may be a smooth or a challenging journey. The good news is that, there is a God who stands at each stage of the journey and is ever ready to give you a helping hand to aid you to a successful end. If I were you, I would seek the wisdom of this great God in your search of purpose. **Proverbs 3:5** says 'Trust in the Lord with all your heart and lean not on your own understanding, acknowledge him and he shall direct your path.' Many are the plans of man but it is the counsel of the Lord that shall stand. (Proverbs19:21) You might have good dreams and aspirations but until they fall in line with God's agenda for your life, you are just working out a self-ambition and in vain. **James 1:5** says "if anyone lacks wisdom, let him asks of the Lord, who gives to all men liberally, upbraided not, and it shall be given unto him." God is more than existence. God wants you to walk in your destined calling. God desires for you to walk in your purpose. God desires that you fulfill the purpose for which he created you. God desires that you make an impact in the lives of people through the fulfillment of your purpose on earth. God doesn't desire that you walk in confusion, knowing not what to do. It's not the will of God that you work in the wrong career and profession. He desires the best of things for your life. God desires that you walk in a better understanding of your existence on this earth. God doesn't wish for you to live a wasted and useless life.

Therefore, I humbly urge you to use every available means through group and individual prayer times to knock at the door of God. I can assure you that your efforts will not be in vain. Through daily interaction with God, the Spirit of God will begin to convince and convict you regarding this reality. The Holy Spirit will lead you into all truth. He is your guide and teacher and He will reveal to you all that you do not know. *(John 14:26) Daniel 11:32b* says that *"but the people who know their God shall be strong and do exploits.*"

May the eyes of your understanding be opened to this truth and may God empower you to affect your generation through your purpose.

FOUR WAYS BY WHICH YOU CAN ASK THE LORD TO KNOW YOUR PURPOSE

1. *Through A Relationship With God*

"Only in Christ can men and women find answers to the ultimate questions that trouble them. Only in Christ can they fully understand their dignity as persons created and loved by God. Jesus Christ is "the only Son from the Father, full of grace and truth." (*John Paul II. World Youth Day, 1993. Denver, Colorado)*

Man's foremost purpose is to have a relationship with God, glorify and please him but with man's fall into sin, fellowship with God is broken, relationships with others are strained, work seems to always be frustrating, and man struggles to maintain any semblance of dominion over nature. Only by restoring fellowship with God, through faith in Jesus Christ, can purpose in life be rediscovered. The purpose of man is to glorify God and enjoy Him forever. We glorify God by fearing and obeying Him, keeping our eyes on our future home in heaven, and knowing Him intimately. We enjoy God by following His purpose for our lives, which enables us to experience true and lasting joy-the abundant life that He desires for us.

You cannot just approach somebody's father one day and ask him to pay your school fees, he will think you are out of your mind, because he knows you from nowhere, so approaching him in the first place was wrong let alone asking him to pay your fees. People don't usually feel a sense of responsibility in other people's lives if they have no relationship with them. In the same vein, although God created all people, he only interacts with those who give him access to their lives. Those who have made him their father, those who have made him their shepherd. The only way, according to Christian teachings by which this can be achieved is through his Son Jesus Christ. That is,

making Jesus Christ your Lord and personal saviour. Jesus said, I am the way, the truth and the life, no one goes to the Father except through me.'
Let's get the following Bible to help us in this regard. verses

"For God so loved the world that he gave his only begotten son, that whosoever believes in him should not perish but have everlasting life." John 3:16

"He came to his own, and his own received him not. But as many as received him, he gave them the power to become the sons(children) of God, to them that believed on his name." John 1:11-12

"If you declare with your mouth, "Jesus is Lord," and believe in your heart that God raised him from the dead, you will be saved. For it is with your heart that you believe and are justified, and it is with your mouth that confession is made unto salvation." Romans 10:9-10.

A careful look at these scriptures point to the fact that it is after making Jesus Christ the Lord of your life that you can start a good relationship with God, your maker. So in your quest to discover your assignment, the first point of call is to establish a relationship with God. God then becomes your responsible father and you become his obedient son or daughter. Every human being, whether young or old must meet this divine criterion before gaining access to a lifelong relationship with God. This is what I have personally believed in throughout my life. You can do same if you feel convicted by the Holy Spirit.

You can say the 'sinners' prayer' as outlined below;

Almighty Father I Thank You for my Life
I am Sorry for Sinning Against You
I Accept the Fact that I Cannot Save myself
and Therefore Need Your Help.
Please Forgive Me of all my Sins through the
Blood of Your Son Jesus Christ.
Lord Jesus Christ, Please Come into my Heart
and be my Lord and Personal Saviour.
Help Me With the Help of Your Grace and
Strenghten Me to Live a Life Pleasing
in Your Sight. Amen.

Remember that, this is just the beginning of a lifetime

walk with God. You would need to join a good holistic Bible-based church, a church that believes and promotes the teachings of our Lord Jesus Christ and allows the full workings and manifestations of the Holy Spirit. You will begin to grow gradually in your spiritual development as you diligently fellowship with God and his people.

After doing this genuinely and wholeheartedly, you have become a true son or daughter of the Almighty God. You can therefore begin to ask him to show you the purpose for which he created you. This takes us to our next sub-topic under this discussion.

2. *Through Prayer*

Prayer is the means by which we communicate with God. We can engage in prayer in a group form or on individual basis. God is a Spirit and one of the ways we can communicate with him is through Prayer. (John 4:24).

One time in the life of Jesus Christ, he was confronted with the issue of choosing twelve disciples with whom he was going to carry out his salvation assignment on earth. The Bible clearly states that Jesus had to actually spend a whole night in prayer before choosing these twelve disciples.(Luke 6:12-13) That was how important prayer was to the Son of God (who is also God). Jesus didn't want to take chances, he was sent by God to save mankind so he knew the only person to lead him in the choice of his team members was the person who sent him to the earth. (John 6:38). And that person was God Almighty, his Father. Jesus had an assignment and that assignment was his God-given purpose. He therefore needed specific instructions about how to carry out this assignment. So he never downplayed the role of his Father in this assignment. He was constantly in touch with his Father. He needed specific divine directives from the Father. He didn't want to fail. Jesus although is also God, constantly, was in touch with his father through prayer. He needed   specific divine directives from the father. He didn't   want to fail. Jesus although is also God, constantly, was in touch with his father through prayer.

The Holy Bible records so many instances where Jesus had to spend quality time in prayer. For example, before he started his public ministry he had to spend forty good days and nights in prayer and fasting on the desert to fully equip himself for the task ahead. If even Jesus valued the place of prayer in the fulfillment of his assignment on earth, how much more you and I?

God knows the exact steps we ought to take to discover and fully execute our assignment on this earth. We must therefore be in constant touch with him to show us the way. God is faithful and he's promised us that if we call on him he will hear us and show us so many secrets we have no knowledge about, including our God-given purposes. If you don't know your purpose yet, I encourage you to talk to God, talk to him in the morning, talk to him at noon, and ask him in the evening. Go to him in prayer in the quietness at dawn and he will surely show you the way. There are deeper wells of talents hidden in you. There are so many untapped potentials in you. You are a valley of precious minerals. To get all these hidden treasures out of you, you must be in constant touch with your Creator. You must get to the mining base of God in prayer. You must churn out those amazing ideas on the table of prayer. You need to coin out those business concepts in the boardroom of God through prayer. Prayer will simply help you unearth and sharpen certain dormant natural and spiritual gifts. Every good and perfect gift comes from God, says the holy Bible (James 1:17). And God is able to give freely to those who ask him in prayer.

GOD SPEAKS BACK TO US AFTER WE HAVE PRAYED

One aspect about prayer that a lot of people miss out on is the fact that, after we've spoken to God, we forget he desires to speak back to us. He desires to give us directions and counsel about the decisions and choices we would want to make. Unfortunately, many people have reduced prayer to a monologue, where we do all the talking but refuse to keep silent for God to speak back to us. I encourage you to make room for a quiet time anytime you pray. Pause a minute or two or even more and listen to the still voice of God for specific divine instructions and suggestions. God is interested in your well-being and cares so much about you taking the right steps that will align you with his blueprint for your life. Get intimate with him and allow him to show you the path to your God-given assignment. Sometimes you don't only need to pay attention to the voice of God, you must go a step further to write down what you hear him telling you.

This must be our attitude and lifestyle. It shouldn't be a one day thing; we must be consistent about it. Keep praying. Never stop praying until you get it all sorted out and also maintain it through prayer.

3. *Through The Word Of God*

The Word of God is the constitution of God for man. The Holy Bible is the ruling manual of God. God wrote the Bible through his chosen vessels by inspiration. ***2 Timothy 3:16-17*** say that ***"All scripture is God-breathed and is useful for teaching, rebuking, correcting and training in righteousness, so that the servant of God may be thoroughly equipped for every good work."*** The point I'm trying to drive home here is that, the word of God was written under the inspiration and instruction of the Almighty God. God chose ordinary men like you and I to write down his commandments for his people. The word of God is therefore called *The Sacred Scriptures, Holy Scriptures, Holy Bible,* because they are not mere human words. They are sacred because they were given by God. In the word of God are found specific instructions, precepts, guidelines, commandments, promises, and prophecies, needed for a victorious Christian living.

"The word of God is at the beginning, the end and heart of creation and the history of the world. It was pronounced at the moment of creation and was completed by the Word made flesh. The Word of God is at the center of everything. It impregnates and gives life to the faith of God's people. It inspires, directs and guides the existence and history of humanity. *The Word of God sprang from the mouth of God, for "In the beginning was the Word and the Word was with God and the Word was God" (Jn 1:1).* The Word of God is the foundation of everything and takes precedence over everything else." *(Second Edition of the New African Bible, Biblical Text of the New American Bible).*

God has laid down certain clear rules that will help man to maintain a smooth relationship with him. They can be termed as the 'dos and don'ts' of life. At the heart of these dos and don'ts (word of God) is a sum total of how we ought to love God whom we do not see. And the best way to do this is to live in love and harmony with our neighbours.

The word of God is God himself to man because in *John 1:1-5*, the bible clearly says that the word of God in the beginning was with God and the word of God was God. This same scripture reference continues to assert that God made all things by the word of God and that, the word of God is also the light and life of men. Hallelujah!

Evangelist Reinhard Bonnke (International Charismatic Evangelist) shared the following text about the Word of God on his official *Facebook page, dated 29th June 2015*:

"The Bible does not tell us what people have thought about God-but what God thinks of us! It is God's inspired message to mankind, and this is why Christians call it 'the Word of God'. The Bible is a book you can completely rely on to tell you the truth about God and about yourself."

So we can comfortably conclude that the word of God;

- ***Was given by God***
- ***Is the light of men***
- ***Created the world***
- ***Is God himself***

The word of God is therefore vital in our bid to discover and fulfill our God-given purposes. Constant reading and obedience to the word of God will open us up to the secrets of God about God himself and about our own lives.

I want us to digest one particular scripture to explain this point. ***Psalm 119:105*** says that, ***"Your word is a lamp unto my feet, and a light unto my path."*** What this means is that, the word of God brightens your way, gives you direction and lightens your path. Your 'feet' stands for your current or present situation and your 'path' connotes your future and the decisions and choices you have to make in the unknown future. So, God by this scripture is giving us assurance that if we stick to his word and hold it in high esteem, he is going to light our way and do away with everything that seem to bring darkness in our way. He will deal with all the confusion in our lives and make things clearer for us. The word of God will be a source of illumination and enlightenment to us. This is what the word of God does.

The stories in the Bible are not fiction. They are the true stories of men and women who lived in the Bible days. Their experiences have therefore become examples for us to follow. Their challenges and the way they were able to come out of them give us hope that if we follow the same path they followed, there shall be light for us at the end of the tunnel.

There are people like Abraham, Noah, Moses, Joseph, Samuel, David, Mary, Jesus and others who received specific instructions from God about their assignments in life. They have become cornerstones and examples for us to follow in our quest to discover and fulfill our God-given assignments. After praying to God, you need to be an addicted friend of the Word of God if you want to see God unfold his plans for your life. The word of God is a sure way to a successful life.

Hear what *Joshua 1:8* says; ***"This book of the law shall not depart from your mouth; you shall meditate on it day and night, and you may observe to do according to all that is written in it: for then you shall make your way prosperous, and you shall have Good Success." (Emphasis mine)***

The surest way to have good success in life is to live by the precepts of the word of God. To meditate on the word of God means, to keep it in your thoughts, ponder over it and keep saying and preaching it till you see the fruits of the word of God manifest in your life.

The word of God will not only guide you to discover your assignment, it will also serve as a master key to opening all manner of doors and unravel to you secrets and mysteries about this life. The word of God will make you a champion and a victor in life. One other Bible verse that speaks to buttress this point is

Psalm 1:1-6 (KJV) "Blessed is the man that walks not in the counsel of the ungodly, nor stands in the way of sinners, nor sits in the seat of the scornful. But his delight is in the law of the Lord; and in His law does he meditate day and night. And he shall be like a tree planted by the rivers of water, that brings forth his fruit in his season; his leaf also shall not wither; and whatsoever he does shall prosper. The ungodly are not so: but are like the chaff which the wind drives away. Therefore, the ungodly shall not stand in the judgment, or sinners in the congregation of the righteous. For the Lord knows the way of the righteous: but the way of the ungodly shall perish."

THIS IS WHAT SHALL HAPPEN TO YOU IF YOU MAKE THE WORD OF GOD YOUR DELIGHT;

· *You Shall Be Like A Tree*

> ***Planted By The Rivers***
> . ***You Shall Bring Forth Your***
> ***Fruit In Your Season***
> · ***Your Leaves Shall Not Wither***
> · ***Whatsoever You Do Shall Prosper***

The last point to note under this chapter is for you to be led by the Holy Spirit.

4. *Through the Leadership of the Holy Spirit*

Let's learn something about this point by using the life of Jesus Christ. It is believed that biblically, Jesus started his fulltime ministry at the age of thirty. So mathematically, Jesus officially executed his God-given assignment within a period of three years. It is recorded in the Gospel according to Luke, the fourth chapter, that Jesus was led by the Holy Spirit into the desert where he fasted, prayed and waited on the Lord for strength and direction to accomplish his assignment; the assignment of dying to save the world. He did this within forty days and nights. The first verse of that chapter says; "Jesus, full of the Holy Spirit, left the Jordan and was led by the Spirit into the wilderness." ***"14 Jesus returned to Galilee in the***

power of the Spirit, and news about him spread through the whole countryside. 17 And the scroll of the prophet Isaiah was handed to him. Unrolling it, he found the place where it was written: 18 "The spirit of God is on me, because he has anointed me to proclaim good news to the poor. He has sent me to proclaim freedom for the prisoners and recovery of sight for the blind, to set the oppressed free 19, to proclaim the year of the Lord's favor."
(Luke 4:14,17-19)

What can we learn from these scriptures?
Firstly, it makes mention of the role of the Spirit in the discovery of the assignment of Jesus Christ.
Secondly, it clearly spells out the mission statement (God-given purpose) of Jesus Christ, that is, *(verses 18 to 19).* In other words, the Holy Spirit guided Jesus Christ to identify his peculiar assignment on earth. The same scriptures emphasises the fact that it is the Holy Spirit that anointed Jesus to carry out all that he was sent to do.(Acts 10:38, Rom 8:11)

"Jesus said to them, my food is to do the will of Him

who sent me, and to finish His work." John 4:34.

"For I have come down from heaven not to do my own will, but the will of him who sent me. This is the will of the Father who sent me, that of all that he has given me I should lose nothing, but should raise it up on the last day." John 6:38-39.

Jesus was a purposeful and focused man (God) because He received and followed specific directions about his assignment on earth.

My dear friend, at this point I don't need to tell you again that you really need the guidance of the Holy Spirit if you want to be able to discover and fully execute your God-given assignment.

THE HOLY SPIRIT ALSO LEADS US INTO ALL TRUTH

"But when He, the Spirit of truth, comes, he will guide you into all the truth. He will not speak on his own; he will speak only what is yet to come." John 16:13.

In this scripture, we are being made to understand that the Spirit is also called *The Spirit of Truth*. It is he alone who can lead us into all truth. We need to know the truth about this life and it's the Spirit that will help us, including helping us know *Our True God-Given Assignment.* The Spirit doesn't guess. He doesn't do trial and error games. He reveals to us the whole truth and nothing but *The Truth.* It's my prayer that as we subject ourselves to the leadership of the Holy Spirit, he will guide us to identify every truth about our purpose and equip us with every strength needed for the task ahead. The Holy Spirit will not lead you astray. He will not get you wayward. If the Spirit was able to lead Jesus on the right path, then be rest assured that with your full cooperation he will smoothly get you to your destination in life. *You Can Never Get Lost, Not Even in the Strangest of all Places If the Holy Spirit Is Your True Guide.* Definitely, the God-factor plays a significant and indispensable role in identifying and fulfilling our purpose in life.

"Man's life comes from God; it is his gift, his image and imprint, a sharing in his breath of life. God therefore is the sole Lord of this life: man cannot do with it as he wills. God himself makes this clear to Noah after the Flood: "For your own lifeblood, too, I will demand an accounting ... and from man in regard to his fellow man I will demand an accounting for human life" (Gen 9:5). The biblical text is concerned to emphasize how the sacredness of life has its foundation in God and in his creative activity: "For God made man in his own image" (Gen 9:6). (John Paul II Encyclicalss: EVANGELIUM VITAE)

CHAPTER THREE

SEEK GODLY COUNSEL FROM EXPERIENCED AND MATURED PEOPLE

"For by wise counsel you will wage your own war, and in a multitude of counselors there is safety."
Proverbs 24:6

One sure way to discover your purpose is through godly counsel and direction from experienced men and women.

Let me use the scenario of the boy Samuel to explain this point. *(1 Samuel 3:1-10)*

So at a very tender age, the boy Samuel served and lived in the house of God. Samuel once heard someone calling out his name while serving in the house of God. Apparently it was the voice of God. Samuel mistook the voice to be that of his master, the prophet Eli. The voice continued for the third consecutive time and in all instances Samuel thought it was the voice of his master, Eli. So Samuel in all three instances runs to Eli anytime he heard his name being called. However, through years of experience,

Eli realised the voice calling out to Samuel was that of God. Unlike Samuel, Eli was familiar with such divine experiences. Eli therefore made it clear to Samuel and ordered him to reply to the voice by saying ***"speak Lord for you servant is listening."*** Samuel did exactly as Eli ordered. Had it not been the timely intervention of Eli, Samuel probably would have still been confused as I write this book (on a lighter note).

What does this teach us?

 Maybe you feel a strong desire to do the work of God, maybe you have a strong desire to become a nurse or a medical doctor. It's even possible you want to pursue music as a career. Could it also be that you have a strong passion to go into private entrepreneurship? Maybe you feel drawn to politics. You could be in any of these categories or other professions. Do you dream of seeking the welfare of others? Do you dream of building a children's home? Do you intend to go into managing a hospital? Could it also be that you are totally confused about your future with no clue to what you want to become? Don't worry at all.

This is the more reason you must seek the counsel of a matured and experienced person. There are people who are specialists and authority figures who have track record in your dream profession. There are people who have travelled the journey you are yet to begin. They may be people in your school, church, community, who have been through what you are going through currently. Don't you think it will be prudent on your part to seek the counsel of such people?

One other lesson we can learn from the story of Samuel is the need to serve others while we wait for our purposes and missions to be made clearer to us. The boy Samuel by then, didn't know his left from his right so far as his ministry was concerned, so instead of being idle and lazing about, he chose to diligently serve his master Eli. Most times, the way to discovering your God-given purpose and mission in life is through your service to others. Don't take such opportunities for granted. Sometimes, God uses such opportunities to prepare us for the greater plans ahead of us in the future. Unfortunately, many people miss this great concept of human life.

Other times, you need to find other talented and purpose-driven people. As iron sharpens iron, so one talented person sharpens another (Proverbs 27:17). If you've got a talent for something, or even if you just hope to develop talent in a field, surround yourself with other talented people and model yourself after their behaviours, practice routines, and attitudes about their talent. Learn everything you can from such talented people.

In your bid to discover your purpose, I humbly urge you to seek the services of a life coach. You need a mentor in your life.

What is Mentoring?

The term *'Mentoring'* has been largely defined by many authorities as a professional relationship in which an experienced person (the mentor) assists another (the mentee) in developing specific skills and knowledge that will enhance the less-experienced person's professional and personal growth.

"Mentorship is a personal developmental relationship in which a more experienced knowledgeable person helps to guide a less experienced or less knowledgeable person. The mentor may be older or younger, but have a certain area of expertise. It is learning and development partnership between someone with vast experience and someone who wants to learn.

Mentoring is a process for the informal transmission of knowledge, social capital, and the psychological support perceived by the recipient as relevant to work, career, or professional development; mentoring entails informal communication, usually face-to-face and during a sustained period of time, between a person who is perceived to have greater relevant knowledge, wisdom, or experience (mentor) and a person who is perceived to have less (the mentee)." (Wikipedia).

A mentor is a person or friend who guides a less experienced person by building trust and modeling positive behaviours. An effective mentor understands that his or her role is to be dependable, engaged, authentic, and tuned into the needs of the mentee. No matter the career path you want to take, the services of a good mentor will be of so much importance to you. Mentors sometimes serve as life guides when we get to the crossroads of life.

A mentor is not the same as a role model even though the two may have some similarities in their roles. A mentee usually has a direct relationship with a mentor but not necessarily the same in the case of a role model. A role model could be someone you get inspiration from. As the name suggests, role models are people we 'model' our lives around. Most times, people confuse the two as being the same, which is not true. A role model can even be far away in another country or continent, but a mentor is someone you relate with directly and in person. Note that a person can be your role model and mentor at the same time. The topic of Mentoring puts much emphasis on having a father-son or teacher-student kind of relationship. Someone you can walk to and discuss pertinent issues with or someone you can call on the phone for specific advice and counsel. For example,

Ron Kenoly, the international Black-American worship leader is my role model in the field of music, but he is not yet my mentor since I have no direct interaction with him. I can read and learn about him on the internet but until we take the relationship to a more personal note, he will forever remain a role model and not a mentor. Don't get it twisted.

What does a mentor do?

The following are among a mentor's functions:

* Teaches the mentee about a specific issue
* Coaches the mentee on a particular skill
* Facilitates the mentee's growth by sharing resources and networks
* Challenges the mentee to move beyond his or her comfort zone
* Creates a safe learning environment for taking risks
* Focuses on the mentee's total development
* *Mentorship* is learning through the mistakes of others. One good mentor can be more informative than a college education and more valuable than a decade's salary.

BENEFITS OF MENTORING
TO THE MENTEE

A Mentee enjoys many benefits including the following:

1. Gains from the mentor's expertise.

   Sometimes a good relationship with a mentor will help you gain access to his expertise without having to pay a penny. A mentor can be more than a school if only a mentee is ready to learn from his mentor's experiences.

2. Receives critical feedback in key areas, such as communications, interpersonal relationships, technical abilities, change management and leadership skills.

3. Develops a sharper focus on what is needed to grow professionally.

   Because of their vast experience in the field, some mentors are able to guide their mentees to focus on more viable and productive ventures. They guide their mentees to concentrate their scarce energies and resources in areas that will yield good results. They help their mentees as a matter of fact to avoid waste.

4. Learns specific skills and knowledge that are relevant to personal goals.

    A good mentor will help you identify other hidden talents in you. Mentors help their protégés to sharpen already existing gifts, talents and abilities. Skills are easily developed through the guidance of a good mentor.

5. Networks with a more influential employer.

6. Gains knowledge about the organisation's culture and unspoken rules that can be critical for success. As a result, adapts more quickly to the organisation's culture.

7. Has a friendly ear with which to share frustrations as well as successes.

    Depending on the level of relationship, a mentor's shoulder can become pillows to his mentee. A mentee can easily run to his mentor in time of personal difficulties and struggles.

The twelve disciples learnt at the feet of Jesus Christ. Elisha had his Elijah. Joshua had a Moses. Timothy had a Paul. *You Definitely Need A Mentor Too.*

SOME MENTORING QUOTES TO PONDER ON

1. I think a role model is a mentor - someone you see on a daily basis, and you learn from them. Denzel Washington(American filmmaker and actor)

2. Cooking is an honest profession where you cannot hide and let others do the work for you. You have to show up, work hard and prove you can do it faster and better. And find a mentor who will recognize your talent and push you in the right direction. Marcus Samuelsson (Award winning chef and cookbook author)

3. The more consistent a father can be or a mentor can be in the person's life and teach them principles of real solid manhood, character, integrity and leadership, the more

consistent you can be in the person's life and teach them those things at a younger age, and then the better off they'll be.

Allan Houston (American basketball player)

4. The best way a mentor can prepare another leader is to expose him or her to other great people.

John C. Maxwell (Author, speaker and human capital specialist)

5. What you want in a mentor is someone who truly cares for you and who will look after your interests and not just their own. When you do come across the right person to mentor you, start by showing them that the time they spend with you is worthwhile.

Vivek Wadhwa (American entrepreneur and academic)

6. I think kids should have a mentor and a role model, but that they shouldn't take one person's opinion to be what we call final assessment or judgment about how life is supposed to be.

Sean Paul (Jamaican Reggae musician)

7. I have a mentor. I have guides. I have a lot of guides. Not a lot, but people whose opinions I really respect and who I will turn to. Jake Gyllenhaal (American actor)

8. A strong mentor can help a young woman find and advance in the career of her dreams that otherwise may have seemed impossible.
Kirsten Gillibrand (American politician)

9. I was lucky enough to have great mentors both in the culinary world and in the world of chefs who became celebrities. Bobby Flay is one of my dearest friends and a tremendous mentor for me. Mario Batali is the same way. They began doing TV a little before me and they showed me the way.

10. Every kid needs a mentor. Everybody needs a mentor.
Donovan Bailey (Canadian sprinter)

11. I love doing what I do. I'm a born mentor. I've launched so many people's careers. I worked hard. Paula Abdul (Singer, songwriter)

12. I come here tonight as a sister, blessed with a

brother who is my mentor, my protector and my lifelong friend. And I come here as a wife who loves my husband and believes he will be an extraordinary president.
Michelle Obama (Wife of America's President, Barak Obama)

13. A guy named Charlie Beacham was my first mentor at Ford. He taught me the importance of the dealers, and he rubbed my nose in the retail business. Lee Iacocca (American automobile executive and author)

MORE QUOTES ABOUT MENTORING

"Children must be taught how to think, not what to think." Margaret Mead (Sociologist, anthropologist)

· "I am not a teacher, but an awakener." Robert Frost (Poet, playwright)

· "The mind is not a vessel to be filled, but a fire

to be kindled."   Plutarch (Biographer)

- "Do not train a child to learn by force or harshness; but direct them to it by what amuses their minds, so that you may be better able to discover with accuracy the peculiar bent of the genius of each." Plato (Philosopher, mathematician)
- "What is a teacher? I'll tell you: it isn't someone who teaches something, but someone who inspires the student to give of her best in order to discover what she already knows." Paulo Coelho (Lyricist, novelist)
- "The mediocre teacher tells. The good teacher explains. The superior teacher demonstrates. The great teacher inspires." William Arthur Ward (Author)

- "In learning you will teach, and in teaching you will learn." Phil Collins (Singer, songwriter)

- "Spoon feeding in the long run teaches us

nothing but the shape of the spoon." E.M. Forster (Author)

- "The best teacher is not the one who knows most but the one who is most capable of reducing knowledge to that simple compound of the obvious and wonderful." H.L. Mencken
(Journalist, satirist)

- "What I've found about it is that there are some folks you can talk to until you're blue in the face--they're never going to get it and they're never going to change. But every once in a while, you'll run into someone who is eager to listen, eager to learn, and willing to try new things. Those are the people we need to reach. We have a responsibility as parents, older people, teachers, people in the neighborhood to recognise that." Tyler Perry (Filmmaker, actor, playwright)

- "Remember that mentor leadership is all about serving. Jesus said, ***"For even the Son of Man*** *came not to be served but to serve others and to give his life as a ransom for many" (Mark 10:45)." Tony Dungy (Athelete)*

- "Leaders should influence others in such a way that it builds people up, encourages and edifies them so they can duplicate this attitude in others." Bob Goshen (Motivational and business speaker)

- "Mentoring is: Sharing Life's Experiences and God's Faithfulness" Janet Thompson (Life coach)

- "Help these boys build a nation their own. Ransack the histories for clues to their past. Plunder the literatures for words they can speak. And should you encounter an ancient tribe whose customs, however dimly, cast light on their hearts, tell them that tale; and you shall name the unspeakable names of your kind, and in that naming, in each such telling, they will falter a step to the light.
Jamie O'Neill (Author)

- "While he was conscious of improving at every

stroke, he did not feel that the other was asserting any superiority over him; and so, though more humble than at the most disastrous period of his downward voyage, he was getting into a better temper every minute." Thomas Hughes (Lawyer, author)

- "Great teachers are great mentors." Lailah Gifty Akita (Author)
- "Good teachers are good mentors." Lailah Gifty Akita (Author)
- "That is the Proctor. He is our Cerberus; he has to keep all undergraduates in good order." "What a task! He ought to have three heads." Thomas Hughes (Lawyer, author)

- "There is nothing I like better than conversing with aged men. For I regard them as travelers who have gone a journey which I too may have to go, and of whom I ought to inquire whether the way is smooth and easy or rugged and difficult. Is life harder toward the end, or what report do you give it?" Plato (Philosopher, mathematician)

"If there is a single factor that spells out the difference between the cafeteria fringe headed for greatness and those doomed for low self-worth, even more than a caring teacher or a group of friends, it is supportive, accepting parents who not only love their children unconditionally, but also don't make them feel as if their idiosyncrasies qualify as "conditions" in the first place." Alexandra Robbins (Journalist, lecturer)

"Imagine what it must be like for teenagers who don't feel they have room to breathe in their own homes. If you are a parent reading this book, you care about your child. If she is quirky, unusual, or nonconformist, ask yourself whether you are doing everything you can to nurture her unusual interests, style, or skills, or whether instead you are directly or subtly pushing her to hide them."
Alexandra Robbins (Journalist, lecturer)

Alternatively, you can talk to a pastor, a teacher, parent or any respected personality in your community. And of course it must be someone who will be in a position to be of help. Preferably, a spiritually or intellectually matured individual, someone you can trust and confide in. Our leaders have smoothly taken the steps we keep fumbling with today. They have learnt valuable lessons which are of importance to our future and betterment. Their lives are stepping stones for us. They have become milestones and examples in our journey to purpose discovery.

Also, you can look out for facilities that address career and guidance issues. Instead of wasting your precious time and resources on unnecessary stuffs you could probably patronise these services.

"Go to the ant, you sluggard! Consider her ways and be wise." (Proverbs 6:6)
The biblical book of Proverbs provides a perfect text of how the lazy should go to the ant and learn from her ways. The ant in this story is a symbol of knowledge and wisdom.

The lazy person may figuratively imply any person who is in need of guidance in any area of life for a productive living. 'Wisdom,' here, could stand for divine insight, matured counsel, godly guidance, and experiential knowledge. In my local parlance, anytime a young person commits a grave offense, there is a saying that goes like 'is there not an elderly person in your household?' This connotes that, where there is wise counsel, foolish and deviant behaviours could be avoided. Of course, not every elderly or old person is full of wisdom, but generally, the aged are noted for their depth of correct discretion and insight. Personally, I have benefitted from this in my life and ministry. Growing up as an active Catholic and for that matter a Christian, I have come across a good number of matured, experienced and anointed men and women of God who have had very significant influence on my life. I have maintained a good relationship with these older folks and they are always of tremendous blessing to me. I have received confirmation from such men concerning the call of God on my life. This in a way brings me a lot of inner conviction and peace. You can call them mentors, life coaches, role models, spiritual parents and God-parents.

Fathers, they say, are feathers that help sons and daughters to fly and soar higher in the journey of life. Their shoulders serve as leaps and heaps for their children. Elders are our compasses when we get lost in the wilderness of life. They are like the white stick of the blind. They are ladders that make us grow taller. They are springboards for a higher jump in life. They are examples for our learning. However, we shouldn't be misled into making these older folks into demigods. They do not take the place of God in our lives.

You are not an island, neither are you the only reservoir of wisdom. Don't be guided by the youthful zeal for self-achievements only. Zeal without wisdom sometimes could end in foolish choices. In all thy getting, get wisdom.(Proverbs 4:7) Seek counsel. Seek knowledge. Pursue wisdom with all thy might. Seek direction. To your zeal, add matured discretion for a safer journey into purpose discovery and fulfillment.

A WORD TO THE WISE
IS ENOUGH

"Those who respect the elderly pave their own road toward success." (African proverb)

"He who listens to the voice of the elderly is like a strong tree; he who turns a deaf
ear is like a twig in the wind." (Nilotic proverb)

"A village without the elderly is like a well without water." (Nilotic proverb)

"The mouth of an elderly man is without teeth, but never without wisdom."(African proverb)

"The wisdom of the elderly is like the sun, it illuminates the village and the great river."(Nilotic proverb)

It is my prayer that God will bring your way, people who will be a compass in your hand on this journey of purpose discovery and accomplishment. Amen.

The next chapter brings us to another important component in our bid to identify and fulfill our God-given assignments. ***Let's Read On.***

■ CHAPTER FOUR ■

THE POINTERS
(PASSION AND POWER)

"Life is monotonous if it has no goal or purpose. When we do not know why we are here or where we are going, then life is full of frustration and unhappiness." (Life Is Worth Living By: Archbishop Fulton J. Sheen)

Have you ever been found wanting in an unfamiliar geographical area before, especially in our part of the world (Ghana) where there are no proper street naming systems in place? However, in this same environment and situation, the mere sight of a sign board that points to your specific destination brings a sigh of relief. In short, this is the work of **Pointers** in our search for life's purpose. They point us to our God-given purpose.

Growing up, I've always had the conviction that I would in one way or the other be involved in church ministry. How did I come by this knowledge? It is the work of the **Pointers In My Life.** I can still recollect some childhood experiences where I used to recite poems and various Bible stories. I have always been involved in church plays, drama groups, church and school choir. No wonder music and preaching are now part of my major careers in life. These innate abilities such as singing, public speaking, acting, writing, have been my **Pointers** in the journey of purpose discovery.

God knows your end from its beginning. He is the architect of your entire being. You are the product of God's mind. You have been specially wired with certain traits, abilities, gifts, talents, that will help you live out your potential to the full to the greater glory of God's name. No matter how desperate you are at becoming a celebrated musician, without the trait of singing in you, trust me, no amount of training can make you a superstar in the music industry. Why? Because your makeup lacks the basic genetic trait of singing.

At this stage I humbly want to ask you this question; what are the activities that you easily do without any extraordinary efforts? You may please find out.

That which brought President Obama into the limelight of American politics apart from hardwork was his gift of oratory. That man is just good at delivering speeches and to some extent this contributed to him becoming the president of the USA, which arguably is the most powerful country on earth. A spoon is always a spoon and not a small spade. Whiles you dig and search for your purpose, I urge you to look out for your dominant and active gifts and talents.

Dede Ayew (Ghanaian international soccer star) didn't need a prophet to tell him that he will be a successful soccer star. He has the soccer make-up in his genes already so it was just a matter of time and training. Those are *Pointers* at work. The Bible says a man's gift will bring him before great men. Identify these gifts, train, polish and nurture them and see yourself finding fulfillment and accomplishment in life.

Whether they are called abilities, talents or innate qualities, they are instilled in each of us at birth. They are those essential elements which combine in each of us to define what we do easily and well. Some talents are so firmly implanted in some individuals to the extent that they control virtually every moment of their lives. Abilities are distinct from skills. Skills are function-driven capacities acquired over time, through practice and experience. Abilities are innate. Manual-dexterity, for example, is an ability: violin-concertizing is a resulting skill. We are happiest and most satisfied when we make maximum use of our abilities. An individual may develop the skills to practice law, for example, but if she doesn't have the inborn talents which make the practice of law easy and satisfying, she will find her work unrewarding (and even, as in the case of many lawyers, frustrating). When we apply our abilities to our study or work, we do our tasks better.

Talk to your friends and family. One of the best ways to figure out what hidden talents you might have is to talk to the people who know you best. We tend to overlook our skills and cover up our abilities, missing out too often on what makes us great. If you're lucky enough to have friends and family who care about you, they won't be so shy about pointing them out. Look at both your strengths and your weaknesses for talent possibilities.

NO HUMAN BEING IS 'GIFTLESS'

There is no human being on earth who is without a gift; no, not one. Each person on earth has been created with a number of gifts, talents and abilities. Never ever think that God made you into an empty useless creature. No. Never believe that lie. You were fearfully and wonderfully made. You are talented. You are gifted. You are resourceful. You are not a waste.

LOCATE, IDENTIFY AND DEVELOP
THE POINTERS TO YOUR DESTINY.

Personally, my destiny basically lies in my *Mouth* (tongue and lips) and *Hands* (fingers to be precise). I was born to sing, preach, teach, talk and write. Almost everything I have been doing since I discovered my purpose revolve around these areas. That's where my power is. I possess special natural and spiritual abilities in these areas. The many people

I have met in life in person and even on social media were through either one or both of these areas, the writing and vocal ministries. The moment I try to be a boxer, tailor or a carpenter, I have entered into a total mess and deviation. Why? Because, I don't possess the innate traits to excel in those areas. So to live a maximized life I need to develop these **Dominant Destiny Pointers**. A lot of people live average lives in career, business and ministry because they have not identified nor developed these pointers to their destinies. Can you imagine the messy situation of how an individual destined and gifted by God to excel as a footballer mistakenly finds himself on the altar as a pastor where he may not be graced to do well? (just an example, no malice intended).? I pity his congregation. There are so many people who have found themselves pursuing careers that are entirely in opposition to their natural strengths and abilities. Their end will definitely be that of unfulfilment and dissatisfaction. There would be no passion and energy, productivity will inevitably be low. I humbly urge you to find time to look within you, pray to God, talk to life coaches and settle these questions in your life if you dream of living a purpose-driven life .

Africa is where it is because many politicians who had no leadership traits in them have ended up in the seats of presidents and law makers. More so, they've not even trained for these positions, so what do we expect?

Do you have an innate desire of becoming a preacher man? If yes, then I'm sure you are likely to possess one or more of these gifts; public speaking, compassion for people, praying, prophetic dreaming, singing, etc. The biblical Joseph and Daniel are classic examples. Joseph became a prime minister overnight through the use of his dominant gift, the gift of interpreting dreams. David through experience had developed a warrior's disposition. No wonder he overpowered Goliath in that popular contest. David eventually became the king of Israel through this conquest. David's ability in playing a musical instrument was another commendation for him in the sight of King Saul. Their destinies were linked to their innate abilities.

Dearest reader, I urge you by the mercies of God to do

a self-introspection. Look within you, dig deeper, and develop those hidden talents. For with them you are already on your way to fulfill that great destiny God has mapped out for you. Thank God for your formal education, thank God for the experiences you've been through in life, but trust me, your life's purpose is more linked with your gifts, talents and abilities, than your several years of formal education.

As you identify these gifts, don't end it there, go a step further and develop them into useful tools for a successful living. To every talent, add skill. To every gift, add proficiency. Work out these raw abilities into finished and better instruments that will make you more efficient and effective in the deployment of your life's assignment.

We have all been given different talents, gifts, abilities. God works in different ways through each of us, and we all serve him faithfully as we use our gifts to glorify him. We should invest the gifts that God has blessed us with wisely. We should use our gifts and abilities to honour God and to bless, encourage and strengthen others in love; (without love, all our gifts are nothing). We should not neglect our gifts, instead, develop them, "stir them up", fan them into flames so that they get even better, to the edification of the church and to the glory of God. (2 Timothy 1:6).

God is so much interested in our gifts, abilities and talents because he uses these gifts in us as channels to reach out to the world. Our gifts are actually an extension of God's hands made viable in the affairs of mankind. Our gifts are instruments through which God carries out his plans and intentions for humanity.

BELOW IS A LIST OF BIBLE QUOTATIONS ABOUT ABILITIES, TALENTS AND GIFTS

1 Peter 4:10 "Each of you should use whatever gift you have received to serve others, as faithful stewards of God's grace in its various forms."

1 Corinthians 12:4-6 "Now there are varieties of gifts, but the same Spirit; and there are varieties of service, but the same Lord; and there are varieties of activities, but it is the same God who empowers them all in everyone."

Exodus 35:10   "All who are skilled among you are to come and make everything the Lord has commanded."

Matthew 25:15a "To one he gave five talents, to another two, to another one, to each according to his ability. Then he went away."

1Corinthians 13:2 "And though I have the gift of prophecy, and understand all mysteries, and all knowledge; and though I have all faith, so that I could remove mountains, and have not love, I am nothing."

Romans 12:3-11   "For I say, through the grace given to me, to everyone who is among you, not to think of himself more highly than he ought to think, but to think soberly, as God has dealt to each one a measure of faith. For as we have many members in one body, but all the members do not have the same function, so we, being many, are one body in Christ, and individually members of one another. Having then gifts differing according to the grace that is given to us, let us use them: if prophecy, let us prophesy in proportion to our faith; or ministry, let us use it in our ministering; he who teaches, in teaching; he who exhorts, in exhortation; he who gives, with liberality; he who leads, with diligence; he who shows mercy, with cheerfulness. Let love be without hypocrisy. Abhor what is evil. Cling to what is good. Be kindly affectionate to one another with brotherly love, in honor giving preference to one another; not lagging in diligence, fervent in spirit, serving the Lord;"

2 Timothy 2:24-25 "A servant of the Lord must not quarrel but must be kind to everyone, be able to teach, and be patient with difficult people. Gently instruct those who oppose the truth. Perhaps God will change those people's hearts, and they will learn the truth."

1 Corinthians 14:12 "So it is with you. Since you are eager to have spiritual gifts, try to excel in gifts that build up the church."

2 Timothy 1: 6-7 "This is why I remind you to fan into flames the spiritual gift God gave you when I laid my hands on you. For God has not given us a spirit of fear and timidity, but of power, love, and self-discipline."

1 Timothy 4: 11- 14 "Get the word out. Teach all these things. And don't let anyone put you down because you're young. Teach believers with your life: by word, by demeanor, by love, by faith, by integrity. Stay at your post reading Scripture, giving counsel, teaching. And that special gift of ministry you were given when the leaders of the church laid hands on you and prayed—keep that dusted off and in use."

1 Corinthians 12:27–31 "You are Christ's body— that's who you are! You must never forget this. Only as you accept your part of that body does your "part" mean anything. You're familiar with some of the parts that God has formed in his church, which is his "body":Apostles, prophets, teachers, miracle workers, healers, helpers, organizers, those who pray in tongues. But it's obvious by now, isn't it, that Christ's church is a complete Body and not a gigantic, unidimensional Part? It's not all Apostle, not all Prophet, not all Miracle Worker, not all

Healer, not all Prayer in Tongues, not all Interpreter of Tongues. And yet some of you keep competing for so-called "important" parts. But now I want to lay out a far better way for you. " (The Message)

1 Peter 4:10-11   "Each one should use whatever gift he has received to serve others, faithfully administering God's grace in its various forms. If anyone speaks, he should do it as one speaking the very words of God. If anyone serves, he should do it with the strength God provides, so that in all things God may be praised through Jesus Christ. To him be the glory and the power for ever and ever. Amen."

Hebrews 3:13 "…encourage one another daily, as long as it is called "Today," so that none of you may be hardened by sin's deceitfulness."

Romans 12:11 "Never be lacking in zeal, but keep your spiritual fervor, serving the Lord."

EXAMPLES OF SPIRITUAL GIFTS

Word of wisdom

Word of knowledge

Discernment of spirits

Gift of faith

Gift of healing

Gift of working of miracles

Gift of prophecy

Gift of speaking in different kinds of tongues

Gift of interpretation of tongues

Gift of helping

Gift of encouragement or exhortation

Fortitude
Piety
Counsel
The gift of giving

Gift of leadership

Gift of mercy

Gift of hospitality

Gift of craftsmanship

HERE ARE SOME QUESTIONS TO HELP YOU DISCOVER YOUR TRUE SELF

What did you love to do as a child?

What sense did you live most with?

Did you see things, make images, did you talk a lot to yourself, were you more aware of sound, did you just feel things?

What are your greatest achievements?

What skills, abilities and talents shine out in you?

What things do you have a real passion for?

What do you like best about yourself?

What three positive adjectives would you use to describe yourself?

What are your fondest memories of being you?

What are your fondest memories of having fun?

What do you know to be true about youself when you are at your best?

What words would you use to describe yourself when you are at your best?

You need to go through the questions above meditatively and prayerfully. If possible, go through the exercise when you are relaxed and not under any form of stress.

BELOW IS A LIST OF TALENTS AND GIFTS

Writing	Public speaking
Singing	Dancing
Sports	Designing
Painting	Drawing
Fashion	Poetry
Comedy	Acting
Art	Computing
Imagination	Intuition
Visualisation	Organising
Reading	Critical thinking
Problem solving	Creativity
Crafting	Weaving
Leadership	Hospitality
Catering	

LET'S DO THIS SHORT EXERCISE

Please take a pen and a paper and list a number of talents and gifts you possess, you can do this at your leisure time. After listing them out, try and match the talents/gifts/abilities with suitable career paths. This will go a long way to help you know your specific make-up and the career path to pursue.

PASSION AND POWER

"Everyone is a genius. But if you judge a fish on its ability to climb a tree, it will live its whole life believing that it is stupid." (Albert Einstein).

Most people live their 'fish lives' as if they were monkeys. When fishes try to live as monkeys, they are living in a fool's paradise and nothing good will come out of them. This is because they are living outside of their natural power zone. To be able to know where God is directing your life and where you can operate at your full potential, you must identify the things you do with so much ease, Passion and Power.

Author and motivational speaker, Jeremiah Buabeng gives this perfect description in his *facebook post dated, 27th April, 2015:*

"Kwamena Hazel is a musician in our church and also a member of the quintessential Accra Symphony Orchestra that was founded by Dr. Mensa Otabil. On a usual day, he looks quiet and almost insignificant until he climbs the stage to conduct the orchestra or the choir or to play the piano. Suddenly, he is filled with verve and enthusiasm that is palpable on his skin. You could virtually feel the thousands of eyes in the auditorium mesmerized by this young man's antics and skill at his chore. That is evidence of someone who is pursuing his passion. He flows! Our own pastor, Dr. Mensa Otabil, is no different. He is by nature a calm reserved man who is not given to much talking....until he climbs the stage to preach. Suddenly, he is transformed into another man. He passionately shares the gift of wisdom that he has been so superfluously endowed with. The persuasiveness of his speech, the flow of his thoughts, the imagery of his illustrations, his enthusiasm and inspiration often leave us overwhelmed after his sermons. He flows! Why? He is operating in the area of his passion. Finding your life's passion is the key to operating at the highest level in life. For each and everyone of us, there is something that turns us on, that sets our hearts on fire, that is clamoring to break out of our souls. It is this passion on which you should build a profession.

Many of us have clear identifiable passions but we have abandoned them for 8-to-5-jobs that is taking us nowhere. Like Hazel, there are people who are great musicians but their gift is locked up in a banking cage somewhere struggling to shine. God did not invent 8 to 5 jobs. That one is our own invention. God invented talents and passions and the freedom to pursue it. He wired us to be on fire for something. It is that something you must commit your life to. No matter how well-educated you are, if you operate in an area you are not passionate about you will not shine. Find your passion and follow it. Don't be side-tracked by money and job security. Follow your passion and in time the money will come." (Jeremiah Buabeng).

Have you ever witnessed a Sonnie Badu (an international-Ghanaian gospel music artiste) concert before? Or what was your observation the last time you saw Lionel Messi or C. Ronaldo in a soccer match? They were passionate about it and they exerted a lot of power, right?

Passionate people normally exert and invest a lot of their energies and resources in the things they are zealous about. Personally I feel fulfilled anytime I get the opportunity to minister powerfully to a group of Christians, whether in songs or through the preaching of the word of God. It doesn't really matter whether I'm paid or not, I will eventually get fulfilled. That is passion. Passion is what gives you a drive in life. Anybody without passion is not living life to the full. I don't know about you, for me, the first thing that comes to mind anytime I wake up in the morning is, 'oh Lord help me to live out my purpose'. I am passionate about singing, I am passionate about preaching and teaching the word of God. I am passionate about helping the sick, poor and needy in society. I am passionate about young people and their well being. *What are you passionate about?*

This chapter has a direct connection with the previous chapter. The Cambridge International Dictionary of English defines passion as 'a very powerful feeling'. I agree with this definition perfectly, no wonder I wrote this book, I have always dreamt of writing a book on 'purpose discovery.' One of my greatest passions is to see people live out their God-ordained purposes. In your search for purpose, remember to look out for your areas of passion and power. I'm not referring to negative passions. Anyone you see around or hear of who is seriously pursuing and fulfilling purpose does that with a tangible amount of passion and a deep seated feeling. They are emotional about it. It drives them crazy. Don't stand in their way when they are at their best. They exhibit a tangible amount of passion and power when they are doing what they are good at. Your passion may not be linked to Christian ministry like in my case, you may be passionate about lecturing, research, politics, international news, journalism, sports, current affairs, business, entrepreneurship and so on. Whatever passion you have, be determined to stay focused and pursue it with every strength in you.

The next time you visit an artist, painter or a sculptor, take note of their imaginative abilities. They are creative. They are fond of picturing images in their minds. In short, they are passionate about what they do so the least time they get is invested in these mental imageries. You can never be a good nurse or doctor if you are not passionate about your profession. A good health worker must be passionate about bringing comfort and wellness to his or her patients. It is sad that many young Africans, especially in my home country, Ghana, are trooping into the nursing profession not for the love of it but simply because of the financial rewards.

Apart from exhibiting passion in this dominant area or field of life, one significant feature is the visible show of a certain degree of *Power* anytime we find ourselves doing the things we do and love best. Unfortunately, a lot of people are not effective in their chosen careers and professions because they lack the needed power for such fields. What I mean by *Power* here is 'an extraordinary strength or skill in a particular field or career'. A clear example of a person who exhibits a lot of power is the world acclaimed athlete by name Usain Bolt. He's by far the fastest human being that has ever lived on earth. The guy has got extraordinary power on the track. He always gives his competitors a good run for their money. He runs with so much energy and his antics alone can scare away his opponents. That's what I'm talking about. Power here, connotes a person's *Niche*.

A niche is a situation or activity specially suited to a person's interests, abilities, or nature. Your niche is what you are cut out for. My niche has to do with church and youth ministry, put me in any other profession and I may disappoint you because that is not my natural make-up or niche.

Your passion is what matters most to your soul. Passion ignites your spirit, provides mental and often physical stimulation, and engulfs you. Passion often starts out in small ways- such as interest in a new hobby, an instructor bringing you new ideas, or trying out a new job. That ignited spark grows into an interest that burns within you, it captivates you. It makes you feel alive, creative, happy, free, and brings a sense of belonging. "The happiness of a man in this life does not consist in the absence but in the mastery of his passions." (Alfred Lord Tennyson, English poet, 1809 – 1892)

If you are searching for what truly ignites you go through a few of these thought provoking questions. They are designed to draw from you what you are passionate about. Passions are about activity, so do not merely read through this list, but grab a cup of tea, a journal and a pen and start writing down the activities, people, and places that come to mind as you read through the list of questions below.

THE FOLLOWING QUESTIONS WILL HELP YOU KNOW YOUR NICHE AND PASSION IN LIFE

What Is My State Of Flow?

This is when you are doing something and you lose all sense of time because you are so engulfed and stimulated by your current activity. When was the last time you worked on something until the wee hours of night? Or missed an event because you could not break free of something you loved doing?

WHAT ARE THE FUN ACTIVITIES IN MY LIFE?

As adults, we often trade FUN for productivity. But what are the fun activities in your life- those things you do just for the fun of it?

WHAT IS MY PLACE OF CURIOSITY?

Many passions start from a place of *Curiosity.* Usually, we all have interest in a certain topic, activity, or event and desire to explore it. This exploration will often lead to a newly uncovered passion. What are the things you are curious about?

WHAT ARE MY HOBBIES?

Many of us turn our *Hobbies* into our careers. The corporate goals, co-workers and bosses can tend to forget that this is something we would do without a pay and at some point in our lives probably just because it was fun. What are your hobbies?

WHAT DO I LIKE TO READ?

What do you like to *Read* about? Are there certain sections of a bookstore that you always migrate into? You are probably very knowledgeable about these areas since you read so much about them or of their type; this is a clear sign of a passion.

WHAT TYPE OF MOVIES DO I WATCH?

What type of *Movies* do you like to watch? Which movies have left a lasting impression on you? Is there a common theme running through your favorite movies? Or have you watched many movies and would you be interested in a movie discussion or review club?

WHAT DO I KEEP RETURNING TO?

What do you keep returning to in your life? These are things you do that you fall back on often. Hobbies you engage in when you go to your 'happy place'. Our lives often follow consistent threads. What are those threads that seem to weave your phases of life together?

WHICH EVENTS EXCITE ME?

What events over the last 12 months were most *Exciting* to you? Which events would you like to live all over again because they were simply amazing and made you feel really good?

WHAT IS MY SUBCONSCIOUS MIND TELLING ME?

Your intuition is your subconscious calling you. You have gone through many thought provoking questions and it is possible that your subconscious is tying together pieces of your life and trying to show you a common theme and passion.

WHAT AM I GOOD AT?

Typically what we are good at is what we are passionate about. What jobs, projects, or hobbies are you good at? What do people come to you for? What do you get paid to do?

WHAT ARE MY SECRET DREAMS?

So many of us have secret dreams that we really want to pursue. These can fall in line with our current careers or be something in a completely different field. What are your secret dreams and aspirations? Chances are if you are reading this you have goals you have been working towards. What are your goals? What do you really want to achieve and are taking deliberate steps towards achieving?

WHAT IS THAT ONE THING
SO DEAR TO MY HEART?

If you have to choose *One Thing* to do for the rest of your life right now, what would you choose? Or flip it- if there was one thing you could never give up, what would you never part with?

WHAT DO I LOVE?

What do you LOVE? What makes your heart beat faster and puts a smile on your face? These could be things about life in general or specific things about you. God has blessed you with many gifts and talents. These seem to come naturally to you, they are easy and enjoyable. What are your God-given talents? Thinking about and doing certain things almost always puts a smile on your face. What is that thing that ignites happy thoughts and makes you smile?

WHAT ARE THE TOPICS
THAT SPARK MY CREATIVITY?

There are certain topics, thoughts and images that spark your creativity. What are those things that make you think, jot down notes, and make you want to drop everything to do this one thing?

When we are really into something we like to talk about it, perhaps a bit too much for those who are around us a lot or just don't share that passion. What are those topics you like to talk about and form your thoughts around?

WHAT WILL I REGRET FOR NOT DOING WHEN I DIE?

At the end of your life do you think there is anything you will regret not having tried? Or are you already living with some of those regrets? These regrets could be pointing to a passion or an area of life that needs to be passionately revised.

Cultivating a passion makes one feel whole. There is a sense of belonging that comes with doing what you are passionate about. What makes you feel whole?

There are times in life when we cannot participate in what we are passionate about and we *Miss It.* What do you miss most if you do not do it?

WHAT ARE MY DAYDREAMS?

Daydreams are ways of exploring or engaging with

our passions when we must do other things or do not have the necessary energy. What do you find yourself daydreaming about?

WHAT DO I WANT TO TEACH OTHERS ABOUT?

We have a tendency to learn a lot about our passions through the things we want to teach others about.

Many times, the positive change we would like to make in the world is a sign of our passion. What positive change would you like to make, how would you make it, and why?

The personal changes you have made in your own life would be beneficial for others to make as well. Are you passionate about this area?

In all of our crazy schedules, we tend to make time for what we love to do, the people who feed our souls, and the things we are passionate about. What do you make time for no matter how busy your schedule?

By now you have a healthy list of potential passions. I am sure a few common themes have ignited you with possibility and perhaps new ideas are distracting you right now. That is a great thing. If you are distracted by potential and a real interest to do something else you probably have found your passion.

Narrow your list down to the few that ignite your smile. This list is your ***Passion Portfolio.***

In our world today, especially in Africa, there are so many square pegs in round holes in our public and civil services. No wonder productivity is always far lower than cost of production. The reason being these workers lack the necessary power and skill for their respective roles at the workplace. They either lack the natural strength in these careers or they have not adequately trained themselves in the skills needed for them to be effective and excel. I have noticed one thing about people in church ministry, and that is, most people want to be 'jack of all trades but master of none.' They don't concentrate on one or two ministries. They are in the music ministry today, tomorrow you find them in the healing and deliverance ministry as well, another time they are in the counselling ministry. They are clueless about the exact ministry they are gifted in and called to. Normally you would realise that such people don't mature in ministry and most times they are ineffective.

What are you passionate about? What one thing easily gets your attention? What is that one thing that you do without exerting much effort? What are you good at? What one activity gets you so fulfilled after you've done it? Answers to these and other similar questions will help you discover your purpose on earth.

MY PERSONAL EXPERIENCE

Let me use a personal experience to drive home this point. One of the poorest academic performance I have ever registered was when I was studying for my university nursing degree. I gained admission into the University of Ghana with a background of a General Arts student and was offered to read Political Science, Sociology, Psychology and Philosophy. My first year grades were superb. The reason being that, I was generally good at the 'reading subjects.' However from second year up to the time I completed, a once brilliant student was now struggling between a second upper and lower classes. So what caused the sudden drop in my grades, one may ask? Let me tell you. From second year I opted to read Nursing in addition to Psychology and Sociology. That was when my woes began. What was the cause? Firstly, the nursing course was so involving and time consuming.

Secondly, nursing was basically a science-biased course, and I have never had a taste for science subjects throughout my formal education.

Thirdly, I just had no passion for the course. So most of the time I was absent minded in class and paid little attention to the practical aspects of the course. The wisest thing for me to have done was to opt out of the nursing course after second or third year, but that never happened and I ended up graduating with a second class lower division in Nursing with Psychology.

Two lessons can be learnt in my experience;

1. Study a course that you are naturally strong at.

2. When passion is zero or low, performance will obviously follow the same trend.

Simply put, I lacked passion and power for the nursing course and no wonder it took me five good years to pass my professional nursing examination. I failed that paper for four consecutive times.

Do you aspire to excel in this life and leave behind a lasting impact and legacy in your career, profession, vocation, and ministry? Then, get engaged in something you have passion for.

I believe by now you are having an idea about what your purpose in life looks like. Having gone through all the processes above, one important thing you must do is to write down your God-given purpose.

WRITE DOWN YOUR SPECIFIC GOD-GIVEN PURPOSE

"I will stand my watch and set myself on the rampart, and watch to see what he will say to me, and what I will answer when I am corrected. Then the Lord answered and said:

"Write the vision and make it plain on tablets, that he may run who reads it. For the vision is yet for an appointed time; but at the end it will speak and it will not lie. Though it tarries, wait for it; because it will surely come, it will not tarry." (Habakkuk 2:1-3)

No matter how good your memory is, it can fail you sometimes. You may forget certain information with time. It is therefore expedient that after identifying your purpose, you must write it down clearly and in plain words. It must be something you can understand. In fact, it won't be bad if you could memorise it. You should be able to tell people what your purpose is anytime you are asked, without missing a word. It is not enough to have it in your mind, write it down on a clean sheet of paper. Post it on the walls in your room. Post it on items where it can be easily noticed. Get used to it. Set your mind on it. For example, this is how my purpose looks like;

"I Exist to Bring Hope, Healing and a Sense of Purpose to People, Especially Young People, Through the Mediums of God-inspired Music, Books, Teachingsand other Acts of Charity."

That is my mission statement!!!!!!

You can also give it a try and write yours.

A well written God-given purpose or *Mission Statement* would be useful for the following:

1. It makes your life's vision and mission clearer. It clears all doubts and confusion.

2. It serves as a guide. It gives you a sense of direction and shows you the right path to take.

3. It puts you on your toes.

4. It will be useful for posterity. It will guide the people who will step in your shoes when you are dead and gone.

    Indeed, "the only way to do great work is to love what you do." (Steve Jobs)

WE ARE GETTING THERE, AREN'T WE?

Now, the next chapter brings us to a very significant point. We are going to explore two things;

1. The importance of knowing and fulfilling your God-given assignment and;

2. The reasons for which people fail to identify and fulfill their God-given purpose.

Come along with me on this exploration.

CHAPTER FIVE

IMPORTANCE OF KNOWING AND FULFILLING YOUR GOD-GIVEN PURPOSE

"God has placed in the heart of every man and woman an irrepressible desire for happiness, for fulfillment."((Pope Francis' Message for the 30th World Youth Day, which was celebrated in dioceses around the world on Palm Sunday before this year's International World Youth Day in Krakow, Poland, in July. Source: Vatican Radio).

1. It Makes You Focused and Gives You a Sense of Direction In Life

2. It Guides You as to How and Where to Channel Your Resources

3. It Helps You Live a Fulfilled Life

4. It Helps You Assess Your Life Well

5. It Helps You Identify Your Strengths and Weaknesses

6. It Makes You a Master of Your Own Destiny and Guides You In Your Decisions And Choices

7. It Makes You A Useful Member Of Society

Let us have a look at the points mentioned.

1. IT MAKES YOU FOCUSED AND GIVES YOU A SENSE OF DIRECTION IN LIFE

I have a very good friend who is a professional teacher. He recently had a degree program in a business related course. This same friend is an estate agent. To the best of my knowledge, this friend I'm talking about is currently at the law school. Three years ago he went into the transportation business and the end of that business was very shambolic. He is also actively involved in church ministry. Sometimes, I wonder what exactly his purpose in life is? He seems to be a jack of all trades but a master of none. I hope you wouldn't want to be like this good friend of mine, would you? This is the more reason you must discover and pursue your God-given assignment.

Knowing and fulfilling your purpose helps you to be focused in life. It gives you a sense of direction and makes you focus on what you hope to achieve in life.

Being focused means that you will not waste your time and resources on things that don't matter to you. You are able to focus your energy, resources, talents, and attention, on the appropriate matters. A focused person cannot be distracted.

In this life, we must learn to be focused in order to live a highly fulfilled life. Knowing and fulfilling your purpose will guide you in the career path to take, the kind of associations to keep and even the kind of marriage partner to choose. If your purpose is linked with Technology you have no business venturing into Sports and Creative Arts, unless technology facilitates your sporting and creative arts.

People who have not identified their purpose are haphazard in their behaviours. They live their lives on impulse with no particular plan. They follow the crowd. They are unstable. No wonder such people don't achieve much in life. A focused and purposeful person, however, is stable and live out his or her life with a specific plan. Once purpose is identified, you would know where you are going in life and therefore be able to seek out the right path to get you to your destination. There are a number of young people in our time who will enroll for every seminar they see being advertised, from business seminars to agricultural seminars, sports seminars, church seminars, health seminars, etc. why? They are simply not focused. It is not a bad idea to have a broadened knowledge base about other fields. However, a clear line must be drawn as to which of these fields is your specialty. You need to prioritise your interest. A purpose-driven life is not a crowd-driven life.

A purpose-driven person is not moved by negative situations. They are not perturbed about unfavourable circumstances because they know what they want in life.

2. IT GUIDES YOU AS TO HOW AND WHERE TO CHANNEL YOUR RESOURCES

Knowing your purpose will guide you as to where to channel your resources. Personally, I don't spend my money on books that are solely based on fields such as fiction, sports, entertainment, politics, etc. Why? The reason being, my purpose in life isn't directly related to any of the disciplines above. I would rather buy books that handle issues on music, Christianity, marriage and relationship, purpose, career and youth empowerment. My choice for such books is as a result of the career and ministry path I've chosen. Even though I like discussing political issues with friends, you would hardly see me at a political rally. I am not a politician so I don't spend my time following politicians. Some other people may do the contrary because that is the career path they've taken. To some, that is their only source of income so politics has become part and parcel of their lives.

The people who have made it in life and are still making impact with their lives are people who identified one or two specific fields or areas and exerted all their energies and resources into them. Bill Gate has become a world figure because of his lifetime involvement in computers. Steve Jobs died a hero because of his inventions and innovations so far as mobile technology is concerned. Michael Jackson was celebrated by the world due to his trailblazing performance and works in the area of music. These and other people have chalked amazing successes in their fields because they concentrated their energies and resources on one particular thing.

My dear friend, you have no choice than to identify and pursue your life's assignment with every strength and energy in you. Don't waste your precious resources on things that may yield no good rewards. A jack of all trades will forever be a master of none. *Wise Up!*

3. IT HELPS YOU TO LIVE A FULFILLED LIFE

One thing about purpose discovery and fulfillment is that, although it might not come with certain financial rewards, it gives you so much fulfillment. A life lived on purpose seeks out to meet the needs of other people. The joy of seeing others happy and comfortable in life through your initiatives is in itself very rewarding, in my candid opinion, that's all that life should be about. Purpose is all about looking out for problems in the society and churning out solutions to them. Our world is full of various human and social needs. The desire of every man or woman living out his or her purpose should be to meet these human and social needs, the ability to achieve this is self-rewarding.

Maybe, you feel called to train and become a medical doctor, a nurse or any health professional so you can be in a position to help people who are in need of healthcare, I would urge you not to give up. Press on with that dream. It would be a fulfilling reality to see people receive comfort and healing through your instrumentality. Maybe, your dream is to establish firms that will seek to help the poor, needy, homeless and helpless children. Go ahead with this beautiful dream. You would be satisfied someday to see these people that you have helped to become great and responsible men and women in the society.

Purpose is simply pursuing the assignment of God for one's life in the provision of certain services and products in the lives of others. It is fulfilling to see the world become a better place through your efforts. There are so many people in life who receive huge sums of money as their monthly salaries, yet they are unfulfilled in life. Why? The reason being they are not following their dream career. Such people are not following the desires of their heart, they are rather being influenced by money.

4.   IT HELPS YOU ASSESS YOUR LIFE WELL AND MAKES YOU MORE EFFECTIVE

Knowing and fulfilling your purpose will also help you assess your life well and make you more effective. We have already said in a previous point that a purpose-driven life helps you to have a sense of direction in life. It also helps you live a fulfilled life. In other words, through purpose you are able to set clear goals and targets for your life. Once these goals and targets are realised or not, it gives you an opportunity to assess your life. For example, if you set out to financially sponsor five needy but brilliant children to complete their primary education, that becomes your goal and target for that period of time. That may be a long term goal though, yet it will still help you to assess your goals.

Purpose, as it has been said already, may be related to the provision of certain social services and products within a period of time. Once this is achieved, it helps you assess your life. Unlike someone who lives on impulse without any specific plan, it will be difficult for such an individual to truly assess his or her life. It makes you effective as well, in that, through previous performances, successes and setbacks, you are able to know the right measures and mechanisms to adopt for a more efficient output.

Lastly, if your purpose is to help raise leaders, you are able to assess the progress of your life's purpose because, at the end of the day you are able to tell how many people you've helped to become better leaders in the society. Purpose generally helps you to assess the qualitative difference you make in the lives of others. The rewards you get and the fulfilment you gain in doing what you love doing is in itself a means of self- assessment. At the end of the day you are able to measure your performance rate based on the impact you made on others. The feedback people may give about how you impacted their lives also serve as a means to assess yourself well.

5. IT HELPS YOU IDENTIFY YOUR STRENGTHS AND WEAKNESSES

A purposeful life will help you identify your strengths and weaknesses. Most people who have fully fulfilled their assignment on earth did that with the help of their innate and inherent strengths, talents and abilities. Many people are confused in life today because they have not thought it wise to identify their strengths in the choices they make. Knowing your purpose will help you realise the true person you are made of and the right fields and career to fit in.

It will interest you to know that there are so many doctors and nurses who can't stand the sight of blood, how can such people be effective in their work since it is inevitable for them to see blood almost on daily basis as part of their work routine. You can't truly identify your specific assignment in life without going through a deliberate self-introspection and assessment. These exercises help you to really know yourself well thereby knowing your weaknesses and strengths in life. Socrates, a philosopher, once said that "An unexamined life is not worth living." This assertion is very true so far as the subject of purpose is concerned. It will be impossible for you to become a world class singer if you lack the basic gift of singing. I mean, if at age twenty you are struggling to make a 'Do' sound then forget it. No amount of training will help you out. I am not debunking the place of skills - training and personal development, for some instances and cases it may be possible through constant training, but in most cases it would be a work in futility. For you to excel in any field of endeavour, it will be expedient and wise on your part to first of all assess your strengths in that area. Failure to do that may lead to low productivity or abysmal performance in the end.

6.   IT MAKES YOU A MASTER OF YOUR OWN DESTINY AND GUIDES YOU IN YOUR DECISIONS AND CHOICES

So many people have their lives under the control of others. It is normal for each of us at a point in time to be under certain kinds of supervision and control due to work ethics and structures. That is a normal phenomenon, but to live your entire life always depending on people to order you about and to tell you what to do and what not to do is completely uncalled for. You must be the master of your own destiny. Be the landlord of your own destiny. Even as a child, although parental guidance is important in the choices you make, at a point in time you may have to respectfully disregard certain level of parental guidance, especially when they are not in line with your passion and dreams in life. So many people in our world today have become slaves and servants to their fellow men. They are ordered about anyhow, even if it's against their human rights. Others can't just make certain vital decisions on their own. They have to depend solely on the opinions of others to make choices. That's a risky way of living. We must welcome the views and support of other matured people in our lives but we shouldn't make them demigods and lords over our destinies. ***It's Time to Be the Master Over Your Own Destiny.*** Know what you want in life and be bold enough to go for it. Don't live by the convictions of others, be led by your own convictions, beliefs and opinions. Be the master of your own destiny. Of course every human being must submit to the influence of the Almighty God, apart from God nobody should have the right to impose wishes and choices on you. As a matter of fact, even God doesn't impose His wishes and choices on us. However, we should be ready to bear the consequences of whatever choice we make in life.

There have been a number of times that people have wondered why I wasn't pursuing my nursing profession. In fact I would have earned so much income if I practiced nursing. Parents and good friends have advised me severally but 'something within me' always said otherwise. Rejecting such views doesn't mean I am being disrespectful, it simply means that I know what I want in life and where I am going in life. I am the master of my own destiny. I can hold myself responsible for my decisions and choices but I can't hold others responsible for the choices they directly or indirectly made on my behalf. It doesn't work that way. Knowing your God- given purpose in life will make you the master of your own destiny. There are probably people who have worked and retired in the banking industry as common bank tellers, I am not trying to look down on peoples jobs, the point I am trying to make is that we shouldn't limit the abilities and potentials that God has placed in us. It would however amaze you to know that in the plan of God, these same people were destined to become managers and CEOs of several financial businesses, but they reduced their destinies to common and ordinary tellers. We don't have to leave decisions like the choice of a marriage partner, career path, field of studies and ministry areas in the hands of others. We must know what we want in life and be determined to follow it to the core. That is what we call **A** *Purposeful Lifestyle.*

7. IT MAKES YOU A USEFUL MEMBER OF SOCIETY

Apart from the personal fulfillment and joy that one derives as a result of fully pursuing ones God-given purpose, there is a certain level of social recognition, acknowledgment and commendation in addition. As stated above, in pursuing purpose, the main aim is to add to the lot of society and improve the lives of others in diverse ways. Purpose is sacrificing your selfish ambitions to follow the plan of God. By doing so you end up meeting the needs of the members in your family, society and the world at large. Having so much riches and personal achievement without any positive influence on your immediate society is not a good thing at all.

The life we live must have a positive impact on the people around us. Life is not just about amassing wealth at the expense of the general populace. Purpose helps us to share in the pains and challenges of others thereby helping to meet some of their needs. There are so many individuals who have contributed immensely to their immediate and larger communities. There are various pastors and other church workers who have given up their secular jobs in order to respond to the call to ministry. There are priests catholic who have left the comfort and pleasures of this life to respond to the call of God. Rev. Fr. Andrew Campbell is a typical example. God has used and still uses such category of people to bring hope, salvation and healing to others. A purpose-driven life kills our selfish desires and helps us to look out for ways to be useful members in our communities. Sometimes, society may not commend you publicly but all the same one's legacy and quota towards the good of other people cannot be overlooked.

Society doesn't celebrate aimless people. Society will never celebrate you if you are not making any impact on them. Society doesn't celebrate lazy people. Rather, society will honour those who through diligence have contributed positively to the wellbeing of other people.

All these benefits notwithstanding, people still fail to discover and fulfill their God-given assignments.

REASONS FOR WHICH PEOPLE FAIL TO IDENTIFY AND FULFIL THEIR GOD-GIVEN PURPOSE

1. LACK OF OPPORTUNITY

A lot of people refuse to live out their God-given assignment because of the lack of opportunities. They complain about the unavailability of platforms for them to roll out their dreams and visions. . Perhaps it is possible to say that a child born into extreme poverty, with severe handicaps, in a small impoverished third world country, does not have, and may not ever have, the opportunity to succeed; but this is not you. The mere fact that you are reading this book puts you into a privileged group of people with boundless opportunities to create a successful, prosperous and fulfilling life. If you ever think, or are tempted to say, that you did not have the opportunity, then you are making up excuses, not providing a legitimate reason, for your failure to create a successful and fulfilling life. There are many opportunities surrounding us all the time. Unless you are constantly looking for them, they may go unnoticed. Be vigilant and always be on the lookout for the advantages or opportunities that may be staring you in the face.

The lack of money is a number one excuse that most people give for not pursuing their dreams. You don't necessarily need money to make your dream and purpose a reality. You need a strong will and a committed heart to push your convictions into realities. Start your dream by living it out whether people and the systems create the opportunities for you or not. Create your own opportunities.

The hard truth is not that you do not have the right opportunities; the fact is that, when the many opportunities that have already come your way were open to you, you were not the right person to take advantage of these opportunities.

Fortunately, whenever you want to, you can become the right person in the right place at the right time for the right opportunity. Yes, whenever you want to finally and definitively decide to choose to pursue your purpose, it is right there just waiting for you to say yes.

Those who are for you are more than those who are against you. God has your back so you are in the majority. Press on. Don't be perturbed by what you lack. Make do with the little you have. That little seed in your hand will grow and blossom.

Don't wait for others to create opportunities for you. Look around you, there are so many social, public and individual needs to be met. Create your own platforms and reach out to make impact. Helpers, benefactors and sponsors will come your way once you stand for something worthwhile. There are more opportunities around you than you think.

2. BAD INFLUENCE/ASSOCIATION
"Evil communication corrupts good manners."

(1 Corinthians 15:33). Many people get discouraged to venture into their divine assignment due to the wrong people in their lives. They feed on the negativity and pessimism of these wrong associates. They hang around with doubters. Their passion easily gets quenched by the evil reports of certain close associates.

Who are you hanging around with, winners or losers? Dreamers or sleepers? Workers or complainers? Many people suffer from being in the wrong peer group. There is a negative comfort in hanging around with other losers, but it will do you no good to associate with people who affirm paucity and mediocrity. Winners hang around with winners so that they can mutually affirm their own right to live out the assignment. If you are really determined to create a purpose-driven life, then you will need to learn to choose your friends and associates carefully.

Did you pick up a bunch of inappropriate information about how life works and are thus subconsciously programmed to be, to do and to have less than you deserve? If you truly desire results in your calling, it is probable that you will have to re-programme and renew your mind. The time to change certain associations is now.

One time in the Bible, God told Moses to send twelve spies from the twelve tribes of Israel to spy the land of Canaan (Numbers 13:1-31). The Lord had promised to give that land to the Israelites. They were to explore and bring report on how the land looked like and whether the people who lived there were weak or strong, few or many. What kind of land was Canaan, was it a good or bad land? Was the land fortified? These and others were the guidelines Moses gave to the twelve spies. Now, this is the report a section of the spies came back to give to Moses; "We went into the land to which you sent us, and it does flow with milk and honey! Here is its fruit." And they continued;"But the people who live there are powerful, and the cities are fortified and very large. We even saw descendants of Anak there." That was the report majority of the spies gave to Moses. A very negative report of course. They saw honey and milk in the land but were overwhelmed by the giants in the On the other hand, this is what Caleb, one of the spies also had to say; ***"Then Caleb silenced the people*** *before Moses and said, "We should go up and take the possessions of the land, for we can certainly do it."* That was contrary to what the other spies said, in fact, the other spies said they looked like grasshoppers before the descendants of Anak. *(Numbers 13:1-31).*

When Caleb was optimistic of victory and conquest, the others were being despondent about the situation. While Caleb was positive, the others were full of negativity.

In life, you need to move with people who have the 'Caleb and Joshua mentality'. If you want to pursue the dreams that God has placed in your heart don't listen to the doubters and naysayers. Don't follow friends who only see challenges but are blind to opportunities.

3. FEAR

This is the big crippling inhibitor that prevents many from succeeding. Fear has cost so many people in life. It is even believed that the Holy Bible has 365 references of verses of scriptures which seek to counter the effects of fear in our lives, which by implication means that, for every day, God is telling us 'not to be afraid.' The primary fear that stops many from even attempting to achieve something outstanding with their lives is the fear of failure. This is truly ironic. People do not attempt great things for fear of failing; yet the simple choice to not make the attempt actually guarantees failure. So you shoot and miss. Every shot not taken misses the goal. Winners know that they will fail often. Ironically, the only reason people are able to accomplish their mandate than others is simply because they failed more or were more willing to accept the possibility of failure than others. This is what Michael Jordan (American NBA star) had to say about failure; "I've missed more than 9000 shots in my career. I've lost almost 300 games. 26 times I've been trusted to take the game winning shot and I missed. I've failed over and over again in my life and that is why I succeed."

Strangely enough, the second biggest fear that prevents people from attempting to go for the gold is the fear of losing certain friends. They may fear that success will change them and change their values.

Fear of failure will stop many from trying new things, but often when there is a real passion, you are unafraid of failure and you learn what you need to learn to get started, gather what you need to gather, and head out to embrace your passion. After all, what you don't know you can learn along the way, fear will not prevent you from fully engaging and loving life. Remember that *Fear* stands for the acronym;

False

Evidence

Appearing

Real.

The thing you fear is actually what God is leading you to overcome. The 'Jesus ghost' that apostle Peter feared, later turned out to be his saviour because the same Jesus gave a helping hand when Peter started to sink on the sea of Galilee. (Mathew 14:27-31)

4. NO FAITH/ BELIEF

To live in this world without believing in something is to cease to exist. People are unable to become all that God has packaged them to become because they lack the fundamental element of faith in God and in themselves. If you fall within that category of people, you need to adopt some fundamental new beliefs about life and about yourself. The greatest sin you can ever commit is to doubt the existence of God. I say this from a Christian point of view. The world we live in was created by a higher being. That higher being is the Lord God Almighty. The bible says in the book of Psalms, the twenty fourth chapter that 'the earth is the Lord's and the fullness thereof.' No matter your religious inclination, it is very weird to assume a disposition that there is no God. To have faith in God is to know that you are limited as a human being and that at a certain point you have to lean on the divine intervention of the Creator of the universe, God. Have faith. It can move mountains. But be very careful where you place your faith. Have faith in yourself. Have faith in your ability to create a self- designed and a God-driven destiny. Have faith in your abilities to have the success you desire. "Faith is taking the first step even when you don't see the whole staircase." (Martin Luther King, Jr.) Have faith in God. Have faith that the same God who created you for that special assignment will help you to bring it to a successful completion. Without faith it is impossible to please God. (Heb 11:6). That is how critical faith is in our walk with God. God told Abraham that he will make him a father of many nations at a time that Abraham and his wife had long passed the childbearing age. They still believed anyway, even though Sarah was pessimistic at a point and gave Hagar, her maid, to Abraham who had a son by name Ishmael with Abraham. The promise delayed for twenty five years. People might have laughed at them. They kept hope alive and believed the more. At the set time they had the promised son in the person of Isaac. "For the vision is yet for an appointed time, but at the end it shall speak, and not lie: though it tarries, wait for it; because it will surely come, it will not tarry."(Habakkuk 2:3)

5. LACK OF EDUCATION/ IGNORANCE

"For lack of knowledge my people perish". (Hosea 4:6). Most folks, even the highly educated, don't have the right knowledge or information about purpose.

I believe quite strongly, in the value of formal education. In fact, I think that the classic, university-level education is a great foundation for anyone who wants to be able to live a fulfilling and contributory life. However, a person can have a PhD in any discipline offered in the best universities and still know nothing about his or her God-given assignment. And you can have little or no formal education and still have it figured out.

There is a specific set of knowledge that is needed to live a purpose-driven life. If you want to succeed, you will need to obtain that knowledge and then apply it to your day-to-day life. You spend your money on so many frivolous things to satisfy some passing fancy. You spend your time learning so many meaningless things. Make a wiser decision: invest your time and money into getting the education that will empower you to create a successful and fulfilling life.

6.   NO PASSION

The average person just doesn't have enough desire to pursue their God-given mission. They are like every other person on the street. They do things ordinarily. Wanting to follow your convictions is not enough. You have to have a burning desire. Become passionate. Light a fire in your belly, in your heart, in your mind for the realisation of your ideals. Feed that fire with the fuel of belief and don't let anyone put it out with negativity or words of caution or even reasonable doubt. The side benefit about being passionate about something is that you get to feel more alive. A life without passion is can be weak life; it becomes a mere existence with less or no excitement.

I would urge to push your dreams. Spur yourself on and be zealous about what you love doing.

7.   NO RESOLVE

Resolve, grit, tenacity, determination, persistence, discipline are major attributes of a winning attitude. You might as well know in advance that when you embark on the journey to fulfill purpose, your tenacity will be tested. In order to succeed, you will need to develop a kick-butt attitude, a firm resolve.

Your determination will determine your results. Fortunately, if you have clearly defined ideals that you are passionate about seeing realized, then your resolve to succeed will come easily. You may need to dig a little deeper in moments when it seems like nothing is going right with your plans. Don't give up. Dig in your heel. Never say never. Resolve to remain resolute in your choices and decisions.

8.   NO PLAN

"If you fail to plan, you will plan to fail." How can you expect to win the game if you have no plan to score goals? The majority of people don't have specific written goals. If you want to succeed in your assignment you have to define your goals. They are the specific objectives you must reach as you proceed to realizing your ideals. Goals are so critically important to your success in this life.

Once your purpose is discovered, it must be boldly written down as a reference point with which you live your life. Specific goals with timelines must be clearly spelt out if you really want to see your dreams and visons come to pass. To fail to plan means you are planning to fail. No successful life is lived that way.

9. NO ACTION

The single biggest reason why most people do not succeed is simply because they don't do anything about it.

People do all kinds of things. In fact, most people are so busy doing stuff that they actually don't take time to examine why they are doing what they are doing. Look around you and you will see lots of frenetic action without any apparent purpose. Stop for a minute and ask yourself, "Why am I doing the things I do? To what purpose? To what end? What exactly is my intention in doing what I do on a daily basis?"

Assuming for a moment that you have the desire to create a successful life, even if your concept of success is not yet specifically defined, are you taking the actions that are necessary to create the results you'd like to have shown up in your life? Everybody has dreams and desires. Not everybody does what is necessary to fulfill those dreams and desires. In fact, most people do not even get started. They procrastinate. They make up excuses why they will start tomorrow instead of today; or they say, "I'll start when the conditions are better, or when my financial situation permits, or when the stars are aligned properly, or when this current project, distraction, TV program, whatever, is finished, then I'll start." NO. NO. NO. Start Right Now! Right now, this minute, talk to God, make a move and create a vision. Create a game plan to enact that vision. Start doing what is necessary. Keep going. Create momentum. Don't stop. Most people never get started; and then, sadly, most of those who are inspired to get started, quit too soon. They get distracted. They allow obstacles to deter them. They lose sight of their goals and ideals. They lose the motivation. They resign themselves to mediocrity. Do you desire a purpose-driven life? Create a vision. Believe in God. Believe in the reality of your vision. Believe in yourself. Stay focused. Never give up. Never, ever give up. If you persist, you will prevail. If you desist, you will fail.

GET IN LINE WITH YOUR PURPOSE

You were originally destined to be a professional carpenter but you've maneuvered your way into becoming a medical doctor. No wonder you treat patients anyhow. You inject your patients as if you are nailing two pieces of wood together. I pity your patients. It's not your fault but it's your fault anyway. You were not naturally wired for such a profession.

Get In Line With Your Purpose.

You were not destined to marry but you are married to three women now with 8 children, no wonder you treat your wives and children as if they are some wild animals in a zoo in Kenya. All your children are outcasts, deviants and social misfits. You are in error.

Get In Line With Your Purpose.

You were never created to become a catholic priest but you are already 7 years in the priesthood. You admired it but within you, you knew God was leading you in a different direction but you were afraid of what people would say if you quit the seminary. So now you struggle with it, no wonder you always feel empty on the altar. You are off-target. ***Get In Line With Your Purpose.***

Broadcasting is not your thing but your admiration for the profession coupled with your extraordinary beauty has placed you in front of our TV sets and you are always messing up. Don't be deceived. Get out of this disillusionment. Discover your true self. ***Get In Line With Your Purpose.***

If you had read a course in the Humanities, you would have been a first class student but your parents said you must be a nurse at all cost and you had no choice. Now you are stuck in the nursing profession and there's no fulfilment in your life. You are actually living someone else's life. You are off. ***Get In Line With Your Purpose.***

Stop Deceiving Yourself and get in Line With Your God-given Purpose. Get In Line My Brother. My Sister, Stop Creating Disorder. Identify your purpose and walk in it. You will live a fulfilled life.

EPILOGUE

Your Gifts, Talents and Abilities are an Extension of the Hand of God in the Affairs of Men!!!!!!!!

People are in dire need of the timely intervention of God in their lives. They expect God to come through for them and salvage them out of their troubles, but God seems to be quiet concerning the pleas and cries of these people. The truth is, God is actually not unconcerned as it is made to believe, because he has created men and women and entrusted into their hands and minds solutions and answers to the unresolved issues of mankind. You are the long awaited miracle in the lives of others. You are the deliverer a particular group of people are looking forward to.

You are an ambassador of God on earth. Your purpose is an extension of the works of God on earth. God ended his original creation on the sixth day of creation. The inventions and innovations we've seen over the years are the ideas of God that have manifested through the application of the diverse gifts and talents of other human beings. God has deposited bits and pieces of himself into each and every one of us. Anytime we step out to fulfill our God-given dreams, we are actually stepping in the shoes of God.

Go out there and make that dream possible. Defy all the odds and fulfill that desire you carry inside of you. Step out boldly. Step out with faith. Gird your loins. Make it happen. God is on your side. Nothing but you can stop you. The world is waiting to hear your story. Make your name count. Don't live a wasted life. You have so much in you for your generation. Let nothing stop you. Be unstoppable. Be unmovable. Set your eyes on the goal. Our world would be better off when you are at your possible best. Don't let that dream in your heart die. The community you live in would be a better place if only you could live that dream out. Fix that issue. Solve that problem. Run that business. It is within your reach. You are more than able. Don't get tired on the way. Push it!!

ABOUT THE BOOK

What this book seeks to do is to guide you through a journey of identifying your God-given purpose on earth. It provides you with basic practical guidelines inspired by scripture and the rich experiences of people that will aid you smoothly to identify your God-given purpose.

This book tries to bring out certain qualities and dispositions that the reader must adopt in order to be able to live a meaningful and purposeful life. You would be inspired to be a winner in life. You would be challenged to go for your best in life. You would be equipped with tools that will unleash the champion in you no matter where you find yourself presently in life.'Purpose Unlocked' makes use of illustrations from the Bible to help you discover your purpose and the true essence of living a purposeful life.

The book is highly scriptural and prophetic. It is interlaced with prophetic declarations and positive affirmations that will spur you on to live the life that God has destined for you, the life of a champion and a conqueror. It awakens the reader's spirit to a higher life of purpose discovery and accomplishment. You have in your hand a book that will turn your world around.

You are about to unravel mysteries about your own life. You are about to discover the potentials that God has placed in you. *'Purpose Unlocked'* is good for people of all age groups but it generally addresses the needs of young people who are hungry to discover and fully execute their God-given assignment. It will teach, motivate, challenge, guide and spur you on to identify and pursue your God-given assignment to the core.

You have in your hand a masterpiece and a bestseller. It is not just a book on purpose discovery and fulfilment; it is a manual to a life of service, peace, joy and self-fulfillment. *ENJOY!!!!!!!!!!*

www.ingramcontent.com/pod-product-compliance
Lightning Source LLC
Chambersburg PA
CBHW022007120726
47992CB00001B/460